Training for Evangelism

by

Richard Sisson

MOODY PRESS

CHICAGO

Library of Congress Cataloging in Publication Data

Sisson, Richard, 1944 —
  Training for evangelism.

  1. Evangelistic work. 2. Witness bearing
(Christianity) I. Title.
BV3790.S56   253.7   79-13324
ISBN 0-8024-8792-0

      10 11 12 Printing/VP/Year 92 91 90 89

Printed in the United States of America

To my wife, Carol,
the first Christian I ever met,
and
to our children, Ricky, Lisa, and David,
the precious jewels of our home,
this book is affectionately dedicated.

Contents

CHAPTER   PAGE

Preface 6

Acknowledgments 7

1. Introduction 9

2. The Need for Evangelism 15

3. Overcoming Our Fears 32

4. Mastering the Three Crucial Issues 45

5. Giving Your Personal Testimony 57

6. A Comprehensive Approach to Presenting the Gospel 67
   Phase One: From the First Minute of Conversation
   to the Discernment of a Person's Need 67

7. A Comprehensive Approach to Presenting the Gospel 77
   Phase Two: Presenting the Five Basic Truths of the Gospel 77

8. A Comprehensive Approach to Presenting the Gospel 97
   Phase Three: Leading to the Point of Decision 97

9. Avoiding Confusing Terminology in Evangelism 115

10. Answering Basic Questions and Objections 129

11. Dos and Don'ts in Evangelism 143

12. Personal Follow-up—A Challenge for an Individual 156

13. Corporate Follow-up—A Task for the Church 173

14. Where Do We Go from Here? 190

Preface

The material you are about to study was for the most part written nearly four years ago. In many ways this book has changed my life. Now that I have taught more than seven hundred people how to share their faith, I am convinced that a significant part of the joy of the pastorate is to be able to equip the men and women of the church to do the work of the ministry.

This training material is still changing my life. In a way, I have taken the course ten times. I now understand that although none of us will ever be able to say he has enough training, every exposure to more training increases our competence and our confidence.

Perhaps the biggest change in my ministry since the evangelism workshops began has been in my place of service. The evangelism workshop grew out of my work as pastor of the North Side Gospel Center, in Chicago. I will always cherish the lessons I learned at the Center.

In the fall of 1978, I accepted the call to pastor the Middleton Baptist Church in Madison, Wisconsin. A new challenge is before me. I am excited about the prospect of seeing the men and women of this church trained to tell others about their faith. As of this writing, our first evangelism workshop has begun. Fifty-two people are presently engaged in training.

As you study the following material, you will notice references to the Center, its Crusader group, and the city of Chicago. I have chosen to leave this material intact, for although I am no longer in Chicago, the principles I learned there are applicable to all churches.

My prayer is that this material will be of some help to you as you discover for yourself what it means to be a "fisher of men."

Acknowledgments

I would like to express my sincere appreciation to Lance B. Latham for teaching me the great issues of the gospel of the grace of God, to Dr. James Kennedy, who first challenged me to develop a training program in evangelism, and to my wife, Carol, from whose lips I first heard the Word of Life.

Heartfelt thanks go also to Paul Kostelny, Dan Fritz, and Fred Mattes, who were the founding fathers of our Crusader outreach ministries at the North Side Gospel Center. Their encouragement was a vital part of the development of this material. Special thanks go to Eileen Depner, who did all the original typing. The difficult task of preparing the earlier edition of this manual, which came out as a hardcover notebook, was borne by Erle and Betty Hungness.

Finally, I offer special thanks to Les Stobbe, Robert Flood, Bill Henry, and the entire editorial staff of Moody Press for their diligence in assembling this manuscript.

1

Introduction

When it comes to the matter of telling people about important information, there are really only two issues: "Is the information true?" and "Is your method for telling someone about it effective?"

If the information is the gospel of the grace of God, those two questions become even more significant. And it is important in telling someone about the gospel to be certain that the answer to both questions is yes. A person can think he is witnessing and know that what he is saying is true but never see the people with whom he is talking come to assurance of salvation. On the other hand, one can have a sure-fire, result-oriented method for obtaining "conversions" and yet not really be giving the necessary truths of the gospel.

In the pages that follow, you will be exposed to an exciting method of telling others about your faith. I have presented the material in this manual numerous times at the church I pastor, and I am convinced that this is a truthful and workable method for training men and women to evangelize.

Scores of church members have taken this training and are winning precious souls to Christ. Our people go out on Tuesday nights to tell others about the gospel and to train others by experience. People in our neighborhood are saved and brought into the fellowship of our church and Sunday school.

In three years our Sunday school has grown rapidly despite the fact that we are a city church with no parking lot and a crowded building.

What we are doing is working. And we have not watered down the gospel message or diluted its offensive aspects in any way. That is noteworthy,

(Use this margin for notes)

The goal of every church: an evangelistic training program that is truthful and workable

9

because it seems that a common practice today is to soften the vocabulary of the Bible so as not to offend people. That is foolish—for the gospel, not Madison Avenue technique, is the power of God unto salvation.

Let me take a moment at the outset of this manual to give some personal thoughts on the two questions we mentioned previously.

IS THE INFORMATION TRUE?

The ministry of Lance B. Latham

The most memorable human being I have ever known is Lance B. Latham. He founded the North Side Gospel Center, the church in which I now serve. He pastored it for more than forty years. He has accomplished more for Christ in the eighty-three years of his life than many entire denominations. He has been instrumental in the founding of the Awana Youth Association, the New Tribes Mission, Camp Awana, and the North Side Gospel Center. He is the human factor in the raising up of forty-six of our own young people to serve on the mission fields of the world. People used to observe that it seemed that every evanglical church in the Chicago area had a youth pastor who was raised and trained at the North Side Gospel Center by Lance Latham.

What has been Lance Latham's secret? He has fallen in love with the truth of the message of Calvary. Moreover, he has instilled the same love for the gospel in the hearts of all who have been associated with him.

The key to Lance Latham's ministry: "I know how a sinner gets saved."

Shortly after I began pastoring the North Side Gospel Center, Lance Latham took me out to lunch and told me, "Dick, I guess I regret that I never learned how to be a pastor. I just kind of fell into it. I have done a lot of foolish things! I have left fathers-of-the-bride standing throughout wedding ceremonies. I have allowed all the kids in the neighborhood to run through my office constantly. When I started the Center I didn't know how to conduct a board meeting, baptize a new believer, print a bulletin, or preach a sermon. But the thing that has singularly sustained me through all those shortcomings is that I know what the gospel is. I know how a sinner gets saved."

A person becomes dynamic when he is sure that what he believes is true. There is incredible strength in conviction. But there is only one truth. There is but one saving Person, one saving gospel, and one right response.

Paul the apostle said: "Moreover, brethren, I declare unto you the gospel which I preached

10

unto you, which also ye have received, and wherein ye stand; by which also ye are saved" (1 Corinthians 15:1-2). We don't need a more complete gospel. We don't need a better message. We simply need to understand what the gospel declares. We need to be trained to tell others about it purely, simply, logically. That is the purpose of this manual. Our thesis is that *a person is never the same again when he has a clear understanding of the gospel, and a logical way to present it, and when he has seen it change lives.* It has been the thrill of my life to see housewives turn into evangelists, introverts turn into aggressive witnesses, and inactive Christians become motivated. All of this is possible only when people know the truth.

How well do you know the truth of the gospel? Right now, put down this book and say what you believe to be the complete message of the gospel. Pretend that someone is with you who wants to know some answers. Could you give him a succinct testimony of how you have been saved? How certain are you that your information is true?

IS YOUR METHOD FOR TELLING SOMEONE ABOUT IT EFFECTIVE?

I have been told that since 1945 almost two thousand churches have closed their doors in Chicago. Churches are no longer supposed to grow in this vast city. It is the graveyard of churches, the death of pastors with ambition.

Our church looks like a converted movie theater. Some people jokingly refer to it as "the shoe factory." No one comes to our services just because he is walking by and becomes enamored with the aesthetic qualities of our structure. We have recently converted our feeble parking lot into an educational building that will permit us to have one thousand in Sunday school. We have almost no parking. Lack of parking is the cause of death for many inner-city stores and shops. But we are growing.

We have a fascinating congregation. The group of people who began this work with Lance Latham forty-five years ago are approaching retirement age. We have a few families in their forties. And there is a flood of newly saved young adults. By a miracle of grace, these two sides of our congregation, old and young, are growing in their appreciation for each other. Their common appreciation for the gospel has given them a bond.

The gospel needs no embellishment

Do you know God's saving plan? Tell yourself its essential issues right now

The "Center" story

Even in a conventional city church, growth can happen when people are trained.

11

We are a rather conventional church. We have preaching services, prayer meetings, and potluck suppers. We believe in the necessity of order, structure, and recognizable leadership. Our members practice separation from worldliness. Our services are built around the expositional teaching of God's Word. Conventional churches are supposed to be vestigial remains of another era. But we are growing.

Churches don't need a revolution in form, they need basic training

A revolution in form is not the key to reaching our cities. Rather, we need a commitment to the development of confidence in our message, confidence in ourselves, and confidence in a supernatural God.

Why don't more Christians have that kind of confidence? The answer is simply that it cannot be taught only from behind the pulpit. It will be developed in individuals as they see it in the lives of the pastor and the recognized leadership of the church.

OUR EXPERIENCE

Young adult ministries begin

Three years ago, we began a young adult Sunday school class with twelve people. At the same time, a weekday Bible class was developed in the basement of one of our families. Both classes majored in clearly presenting the gospel of grace. People were saved. In the course of that first year, our young adult class grew to about sixty-five.

Something missing

Yet something was missing. Our people began to take the truth for granted. They did not feel confident in witnessing. Instead of winning people to Christ, they would invite them to come to Sunday school or the Bible class. Just at that time I was privileged to hear James Kennedy at the annual Pastors' Conference at Moody Bible Institute. His message was electrifying. It occurred to me that our people had enough knowledge to recall the message when they heard it, but not enough to reproduce it by themselves. I began to wrestle with two questions: What is distinctive about the gospel message? And could God use me to develop a training program for evangelism that effectively incorporated the distinctives of the gospel?

Dr. Kennedy's message

Our first training program

After much preparation, we announced that we would be holding a fourteen-week series of evangelism workshops on Tuesday evenings. Part of the instruction would be in the classroom for training in content. For the other part we would take trainees into people's homes so that they could see real evangelism taking place.

On the first night, about thirty people showed up. I was thrilled! It did not take long, however, for the initial enthusiasm of some to wear off. The intensity of our training program had its effect as, one by one, people dropped out. But at the same time those who stayed with it began to change. Truly, it is awesome to see what happens to a man who sees for himself that the gospel is the power of God unto salvation.

Out of that original group of thirty, a dozen finished the training. They became the nucleus for the evangelistic thrust of our church.

After the first workshop, we all felt a need to maintain our momentum. A group was begun which called itself the "Crusaders." Its purpose was to develop and implement a strategy for reaching the Chicagoland area with the gospel of Christ. The prerequisite for joining the Crusaders was simply to take our evangelism workshop training. Through the creative energies of this group we have come up with a wide range of evangelistic thrusts, including street meetings, flea-market evangelism, door-to-door evangelism, tract distribution, telephone evangelism, newspaper evangelism, and film evangelism.

Imagine my thrill as a pastor in meeting with twenty-five to forty dedicated young adults at the monthly Crusader meeting. Instead of playing bingo or listening to boring financial reports, we spend every minute of our meeting time discussing how we can do more to reach Chicago with the glorious message of Calvary.

We have now conducted eight entire series of workshops, and several hundred people have been thoroughly trained. Many are now serving as trainers. Each Tuesday night, our people are given three calls to make in neighborhood homes, and virtually every week people are led to a saving knowledge of Christ.

But more than any of those things, there looms one supreme result of our evangelism training: Every one of our people is absolutely persuaded that we can affect the destiny of Chicago. The motto of our church has become "We can!" We wear that motto proudly on our lapel pins. We can be part of what well may be God's last outpouring of mercy on a great city before judgment comes. We can win precious souls to Christ. We can "reign in life" (Romans 5:17). We can, by the grace of God, be kings who are in control of our passions. We can have an impact on people's lives.

Our nucleus—a dozen trainees

The Crusaders are formed to implement a strategy for Chicago outreach

Training has produced a gigantic optimism—we can affect the destiny of Chicago

**To the degree
people believe
that they are part
of a great work,
they will make
great sacrifices**

Our city does not suffer from lack of churches. But it—and every other city—lacks churches whose people live with an exciting sense of destiny. One of our church tenets is that to the degree that people are persuaded that they are part of a great work, they are willing to make great sacrifices for that work.

The Bible says much about the greatness of our mission. Like Nehemiah of old, who was responsible for constructing the wall of Jerusalem, we need to say: "I am doing a great work, so that I cannot come down" (Nehemiah 6:3). Like the angels of the Bethlehem hills, we need to be convinced that the gospel is "good tidings of great joy" (Luke 2:10). We need to believe like Paul that "a great door and effectual" is open (1 Corinthians 16:9). Like the writer of Hebrews we should thrill to "so great salvation" (Hebrews 2:3). Finally, along with Malachi, we believe that our God is "a great King" (Malachi 1:14).

We offer this training manual to you in the hope that it will be a tool in the hand of a mighty God to *persuade you of the exciting part that you can play in the most staggering and electrifying task that any human could undertake:* reaching a sinful world with the good news that Christ died for our sins (1 Corinthians 15:3).

**Study these
verses**

As you begin this manual on evangelism, we ask you to do so only after you have saturated yourself with the truths of two mighty verses that have become the theme verses of our Crusader group: "And Jesus looking upon them saith, With men it is impossible, but not with God: for with God all things are possible" (Mark 10:27). "They that sow in tears shall reap in joy. He that goeth forth and weepeth, bearing precious seed, shall doubtless come again with rejoicing, bringing his sheaves with him" (Psalm 126:5-6).

2

The Need for Evangelism

SOLDIERS OR SPECTATORS?

Our lives were meant to be full. And fullness is directly related to fruitfulness. To the very degree that we are fruitful (that is, to the very degree that we see the life of Christ reproduced in us and in others), life becomes profoundly meaningful. Yet it has been estimated that only four out of every hundred Christians know how to tell others about their faith with confidence and precision. Does that shock you? It should, because the world will never be reached for Christ by 4 percent of the church. At that rate, we are doomed to failure. It is shocking also because it indicates an incredible ignorance about God's master plan for evangelism.

No brilliant theologian or perceptive professor of evangelism has been able to improve on our Savior's strategy: "Follow me, and I will make you fishers of men" (Matthew 4:19). Evangelism is not supposed to be a specialty sport for a few master fishermen. It should be the fundamental concern of all who follow Christ. Figuratively, therefore, when one is born again through faith in Jesus Christ, he is given citizenship papers in the Kingdom of heaven and a fishing pole for the sea of humanity.

In the book of Acts we see God's plan in its simplicity. The eighth chapter begins with the dispersion of the church caused by the persecution that accompanied Stephen's martyrdom. Luke says, "They were all scattered abroad . . . except the apostles [who stayed in Jerusalem]" (Acts 8:1). Verse four gives us the dramatic result, *"They that were scattered abroad went every where preaching the word."*

Only four out of one hundred can tell others about their faith

The Savior's strategy: "Follow me, . . . [become] fishers of men"

15

Evangelism: a spectator sport

Two thousand years of church history have gone by since that first scattering. The church is different now. It is paying a fearful price for that difference. Perhaps the greatest tragedy is the way evangelism has become a spectator sport. Pastors with whom I talk tell the same sad story. Their people will come to church often if the right Christian celebrity is giving a sacred concert or if there is a film that has plenty of action.

Recently, a concert series sponsored by a number of evangelical churches in our area was canceled. The three-thousand-seat auditorium they were planning to use was not big enough to attract the evangelical artists who are in such awesome demand that they can selectively limit themselves to concerts of five thousand or more people. As has been said often, the church of the twentieth century resembles a professional football game. Seventy thousand spectators desperately in need of exercise watch twenty-two men on the field who are desperately in need of rest.

As the concept of church participation has changed, so has the concept of Christian responsibility. It seems that to many people a local congregation is successful when it fills the church building. When that attitude predominates the idea begins to develop that church attendance is *my service* for Christ rather than *my preparation for service* for Christ.

Tragic church philosophy— "attendance is my service" rather than "attendance is my preparation for service"

More often than not, people are judged to be spiritually mature simply because they come to all the meetings. When that mentality infects a church, one proves his devotion to Christ by enduring the preaching rather than by feasting upon the Word, which can then be shared with others throughout the week.

Picture now what the church was intended to be. The following chart shows the ministries of a balanced church:

EVANGELISM	EDIFICATION	FELLOWSHIP	SERVICE
Going to the lost	Worship	Sharing our lives and the life of Christ with each other	Meeting the needs of people—both Christians and non-Christians
Giving them the gospel where they are	Instruction		
Bringing them into the fellowship of God's people	Prayer	Developing a commonness of concerns	

A church like this needs participation from every member. This, of course, is the ideal. When Christians become spectators instead of partici-

16

pants, the picture is distorted. The church takes on a new appearance:

EVANGELISM	EDIFICATION	FELLOWSHIP	SERVICE
Supporting a pastor or a minister of evangelism who can reach the lost	Putting on a great show for spectators on Sunday	Enjoying the exclusive company of a few select friends	Putting money into the offering plate

As I look at the above charts, I am convinced of two things. First, the world will never be reached by clergymen. Second, even if the world were reached by clergymen, the church would not be the church.

The world will not be reached by clergymen

The point is that when people become participants in the evangelistic outreach of the church, it affects more than evangelism. Worship takes on new significance. Not only do church members have more of a desire to recharge their spiritual batteries, but they also want personally to praise the Lord for the miracles they have seen Him work in the lives of people. Fellowship becomes a vital thing because they are constantly opening up their hearts to new friends for whom they feel an acute personal responsibility. Service takes on new meaning. In Chicago, for example, the people we are winning to Christ have all kinds of needs. It is the thrill of my life as a pastor to see our church members mobilized for the meeting of those needs.

Evangelism affects the total life of the church

How can laymen reach their world? There are four conditions that must be met if this exciting possibility is to be realized.

Four conditions if the world is to be reached by laymen

First, laymen must see that they are ministers of Christ and as responsible for the lost as the pastor is. I am convinced that that is the real key to everything. The church is the community of saints. They have a need for pastoral leadership, certainly, but everyone in the community shares equally the responsibility to be Christ's ambassadors.

1. Accept total responsibility

Second, laymen must be effectively trained in evangelism. If the pastor fails here, he has failed completely. Many large churches in the great metropolitan centers of our country have gifted preachers who share the Word passionately and sincerely with congregations of thousands, week after week. Yet their communities are still unevangelized. It is my conviction that if those same gifted men were to concentrate on training their laymen, they would see a dramatic increase in the effectiveness of their ministries. Training is the only cure for people who otherwise would rely on excuses.

2. Have sufficient training

3. Believe that discipleship means evangelism

Third, laymen must accept the fact that the call to be Christ's disciples is the call to become fishers of men. There are some who think that the church's exclusive task is to promote the deeper life. Their belief is that if we take care of our own personal holiness, God will use us to build His church. He will send people our way. People will see our lives and be motivated to trust Christ. That is tragically shortsighted. Christ says: "Go into the highways and hedges and compel them to come in" (Luke 14:23). You cannot follow Christ and forget aggressive evangelism. He said, "Follow me, and I will make you fishers of men" (Matthew 4:19). Our Lord's last words on earth were these: "Ye shall receive power, after that the Holy Ghost is come upon you: and ye shall be witnesses unto me" (Acts 1:8).

4. See evangelism in action

No man is the same after he has seen for himself a person trust Christ

Fourth, laymen must actually see evangelism happening by watching someone witness. No man is ever the same again after he has been trained to see clearly the great issues of the gospel and after he has seen, with his own eyes, someone's life change as that person responds in belief to the message of the cross.

Training by doing is the missing link in most evangelistic training programs. You will not learn to evangelize merely by reading this book. You must see its principles work as you ring doorbells and actually tell your acquaintances about Christ. I urge you to study this material with someone who has already overcome his fears and is sharing his faith regularly.

THE ROLE OF EVANGELISM IN A SELF-DESTRUCTING SOCIETY

What really affects society?

There is much talk these days about the "full-orbed gospel." Many are suggesting that we are not going to change society without becoming involved in welfare programs, slum renovations, drug abuse clinics, and a thousand other social arenas. They say that social concerns make the gospel full-orbed.

Dr. Dave Breese

But their thinking is just backward. It is the gospel that makes social reform possible. Dr. Dave Breese, president of Christian Destiny, has said: "When the gospel of grace becomes 'full-orbed' by adding anything to its exclusive message—Christ died for our sins—it ceases to be the gospel!" It is only as men in all walks of life respond to the message of Calvary that change comes to society. Evangelism, then, is the key to social change.

Chuck Colson

Charles Colson received nationwide notoriety as the chief mastermind behind the "dirty tricks" of the recent Nixon administration. For his activities he served seven months in a federal penitentiary. Before he was in prison, Mr. Colson received Jesus Christ as his Savior. As his best-selling book, *Born Again,* mightily affirms, his life began to change. He developed a remarkable appetite for the Word of God. At the same time, his eyes were opened to the futility of the rehabilitation programs of the federal prison system and the hopelessness and despair of countless thousands of prisoners.

After Colson was released, his burden to minister to prisoners in the name of Christ and see inmates changed by the gospel became irresistible. He developed an organization to reach prisoners nationwide with Christ. The success of Colson and his associates has been phenomenal. His work is a demonstration that a handful of dedicated Christians who share the gospel can do more to rehabilitate hard-core criminals than millions of government dollars. He has shown that evangelism is the key to changing men's behavior.

Dr. John Whitcomb

Dr. John Whitcomb, professor of theology at Grace Seminary, offers further evidence of the importance of evangelism. Dr. Whitcomb's specialty is the study of biblical creationism. That is an awesome subject with profound implications. Evolutionists teach that the universe was created by chance through the process of natural selection over the course of billions of years. Their theory is just that—a theory, and the evidence to support it is woefully lacking. Yet nearly every science professor in our schools and universities teaches it as fact. Probably no recognized graduate school in the country would grant a Ph.D. to anyone who advocates creationism.

For years, much of the evangelical scientific community made concessions to the secular community, hoping both to gain their respect and to demonstrate that Christianity is scientifically credible. That approach failed dismally. The only secular scientists who changed their evolutionary bias were those who were saved through faith in Christ's blood. Dr. Whitcomb observed that, and concluded that the study of origins is really a religious, not a scientific, question. The ruler of this world has blinded men's hearts and minds. They cannot see because they will not see. No man will be able to understand the origins of the universe until he accepts God's revelation. The Bible says,

19

"Through faith we understand that the worlds were framed by the word of God" (Hebrews 11:3).

If we hope, therefore, to convince men of the truth of creation, we must win them to Christ. Evangelism is the key to changing men's minds.

Dr. Francis Schaeffer

Dr. Francis Schaeffer of L'Abri, in Switzerland, contends that the absence of biblical absolutes explains the disintegration of Western thought in philosophy, theology, and the arts. He, too, teaches that the only solution to man's dilemma is the truth of the gospel.

My own experience

My own experience as an urban pastor bears this out. I have had many wonderful experiences in leading men and women to Christ over the past years. All of them confirm the fact that Christ is the answer to all of society's failings and frustrations. One couple stands out in my mind. They lived together in what they felt was deep love. Soon they discovered they had very little in common to hold their relationship together. They began to get hurt and angry with each other. Finally they separated, vowing never to see each other again. Just two weeks after the separation, the young lady was saved. Her first thought was to tell "the guy she never wanted to see again" about the gospel. The change in her life and the glow on her face were so real and irresistible that he soon became a Christian as well. They began to go steady again. They conducted their courtship in the most God-honoring, discreet manner. Most important, they discovered that in their mutual love for Christ they had a commonness that brought unity to every area of their relationship. Ultimately they were united in marriage. Now they are fruitful members of our Crusader group and very happy. Evangelism is the key to family problems and social relationships.

I don't know how many pastors have former heroin addicts in their flock. I do. Several have been won to Christ through a wonderful Bible study that meets in the basement of one of our families. Our record is not perfect. Heroin is not an easy problem to solve. Yet this I know: the gospel of Christ is the most effective cure known to man for this type of addiction.

Almost all the young adults at our church who have recently been saved have trusted Christ only after they have tried just about everything else. Many have already suffered the misery of dissolved marriages. Some singles have tried living together. Some have had abortions. Others have attempted suicide. Many have been alcoholics. Most had very low self-images. None was satisfied. They had taken many roads but they had all arrived at despair. But the gospel changed everything for them.

I am not saying that believing the Gospel automatically solves all problems. It doesn't. Becoming a Christian is not the same thing as becoming sinless. A Christian is a sinner who is redeemed and becoming more like Christ all the time. Most important, a Christian is one who has a motive for living a new kind of life—the love of Christ.

If you think America is in sad shape and wonder what you can do, convince yourself that you can do something about it. The very first step is to learn how to share your faith. That may seem relatively small, but sometimes the least we can do is also the most we can do. Have you ever felt that way about prayer?

THE EXCITING POTENTIAL OF GROWTH THROUGH MULTIPLICATION

Recent studies conclude that there are probably between forty and fifty million evangelicals in our country today. That means that if every Christian led just four people to Christ in the next two years, our entire country would be evangelized. That boggles the mind. Not only is total evangelization a possibility, but it is also precisely what the Lord Jesus Christ expects of His church. It would certainly change civilization, but it would change the church as well.

Do you have any idea what happens to a local congregation when its people are evangelizing week after week? The effects are astounding. I was privilieged to pastor a Nebraska church that began with nine families. In several years, the congregation had grown to two hundred people. We saw many saved, and it was a wonderful experience. But perhaps the most amazing part of all was that our congregation began to *expect* people to respond to the gospel. Evangelism was becoming a natural part of our lives. People who became part of our work from other evangelical congregations would observe, "Why, you actually *expect* people to trust Christ, both in your services and in your Bible studies!" Many came from churches where if anyone had been saved, the whole congregation would have fainted!

Yet it was not until I came to the North Side Gospel Center that I became aware of the possi-

An evangelizing church is exciting

21

**My greatest thrill
as a pastor**

**If growth by
multiplication is
possible, *one*
church can affect
an entire city**

**Two commitments
in our training**

**The real
"optimists' club"**

bility that training evangelists was really my main job as a pastor. Without question *I affirm boldly that the excitement of being able to train others to evangelize, and thus to see others far outstrip me in their ability to lead people to Christ, has been the greatest thrill I've ever known in ten years of ministry.*

All of this leads to an amazing fact: *Because growth by multiplication is possible, one church that is functioning rightly has the potential of reaching an entire city.* Here, at the outset of your study of our basic evangelism workshop material, consider this carefully: The world is reachable. Your city is reachable. If we can get the job done in Chicago, in an ethnically diverse area of the city, in a church facility that offers no parking, there is great hope for you, wherever you may be located.

A church is changed by evangelism training and growth through multiplication. In our church we can never keep up with all the new faces and names. Wouldn't that be a delightful problem to have? Special activities and follow-up committees are designed to bring newborn believers into the fellowship of the church. They are urged to register for one of the fourteen-week evangelism workshops we hold each spring and fall. After they have completed basic training, we urge them to think about making two commitments. First, we ask them to commit every Tuesday night of the next year to personal evangelism. Second, we invite them to become part of our Crusader group, which meets monthly to plan and execute a strategy for reaching our area with the gospel of Christ.

The effects of evangelism training on our church have been phenomenal. We have experienced amazing growth, unity of purpose, and increasing faith in the Lord's ability. Best of all, our people know and believe the possibility of our reaching the entire city with the gospel, and we are committed to seeing it happen as our church grows by multiplication.

What does training in evangelism do for a Christian? The Bible tells us to "sanctify the Lord God in [our] hearts: and be ready always to give an answer to every man that [asks] a reason of the hope that is in [us] with meekness and fear" (1 Peter 3:15). When a person knows how to communicate his faith and has seen it work personally in the lives of others, he cannot help becoming an optimist. He feels that he is the steward

22

of the most priceless commodity in the world. He believes that he holds destiny in his hands. He senses that he has been given gold in a bankrupt society and told to share it. He knows that he has been given the Water of Life in a desert and told to pour it out for thirsty hearts. Paul had this sensation of having received a priceless treasure that needed to be shared when he said: "But as we were allowed of God to be put in trust with the gospel, even so we speak; not as pleasing men, but God, who trieth our hearts" (1 Thessalonians 2:4).

A DAY OF UNPARALLELED OPPORTUNITY

William J. Petersen has written a helpful book called *Those Curious New Cults,* (revised edition, New Canaan, Conn.: Keats, 1976). In it he explains why America of the 70s has fallen like a piece of overripe fruit to the cultists. Our society has been transformed from a state of scientific optimism to irrational mysticism in a mere generation. Mr. Petersen takes us back to 1963 as the watershed year for this radical shift. He relates six crises of 1963 that permanently altered our society. The first crisis was when President Kennedy was assassinated in Dallas. Journalists called this tragedy "the end of Camelot." Kennedy had assembled the greatest young minds of the day to pool their resources to solve the world's problems. Suddenly all was changed. The era of political optimism had come to an end. Americans would never again believe that there are political answers to mankind's deepest problems.

A second crisis was when Timothy Leary became famous for teaching that people could find God through drugs. "Tune in, turn on, and drop out" became a popular slogan. Overnight, *LSD* became a household word. Support for drugs was being given by a professor of one of the most prestigious schools in the country.

Crisis number three came when the Beatles emerged from England. Soon men on both sides of the Atlantic would be wearing the Beatles' characteristic hairstyles. The Beatles dominated the thinking processes of a whole generation of young people. It could never be said again that family or church played the dominant role in shaping the destiny of a generation of teenagers.

The fourth crisis Mr. Petersen names came when the Supreme Court, in a case involving the state of Pennsylvania, ruled against allowing

Astounding changes have taken place in our society since 1963

No more political optimism

"Tune in, turn on, and drop out"

Beatlemania

School closed to prayer

23

prayer in public schools. This was a great triumph for the atheists in our land, who began to flex their political muscle.

Honest to God

Another crisis came when Bishop John Robinson, of the Church of England, wrote his book *Honest to God*. Honesty, he said, forced him to conclude that outside of the human mind there is no objective being called God. God is simply the most ultimate concern of our lives. God is within, not without. He stated that the need of the hour was for a religionless Christianity. This, of course, was shocking because it came not from an atheist but from a distinguished churchman. Actually, it served only to expose the obvious—that much of Christendom had long ceased to be Christian.

Mr. Petersen refers to one final crisis occuring in 1963. That year marked the low ebb of the influence of main-line denominations in our society. The church was stagnant and complacent. It had lost sight of its mission. It had nothing to offer a groping world. Soon evangelicals would make themselves felt in incredible ways. The next fifteen years would be the greatest days for evangelism in two hundred years.

The birth of the New Left

Out of the events of 1963 new trends began to emerge. The new interest in drugs became a whole subculture. Then there came the radicalism of the New Left, which grew out of the Free Speech movement in Berkeley, California. Soon the country was alive with activity over the Viet Nam issue. Within a few years, and with the help of a few bombings and suicides, despair began to set in. In the wake of this despair, the Jesus Movement brought temporary relief. However, because of its lack of a solid base, it did not last.

Eastern mysticism holds sway

Now our country has turned to mysticism. It is the theology of escape. People are told to crucify their intellects and deepen their sensations. Eastern cults are teaching men how to escape the consequences of guilt. They are taught to stop thinking and start meditating. Yet they can never deal sufficiently with the problem of guilt. Eastern mysticism offers no permanent peace, no real forgiveness. People are still in despair. It is time for Christianity to shine. The same climate that has nurtured cults throws the door wide open to the gospel.

What a great day to be a Christian!

If ever there was a day when it is exciting to be a Christian, it is today. The forces of evil are everywhere. Such is the nature of our society that man can no longer stay neutral behind an empty shell of moral living. The very decadence of our world is forcing men to choose. And never before have the choices been so clear.

WARNING: A PICTURE OF THE FUTURE IF WE FAIL

We must remember that the unparalleled opportunity to evangelize that we now enjoy has grown out of a chaotic moral, political, social, and economic climate that has been caused by the abandonment of divine absolutes. As Dr. Francis Schaeffer has often stated, when society abandons God's absolutes, society becomes absolute. But the absolutes of a godless society are arbitrary. They are designed to serve the interests of the humanists and their power system. The masses accept their power structure, Schaeffer says, for even tyranny is preferable to anarchy.

The picture from history is clear—the dissolution of a powerful state begins with abandonment of ideals, proceeds with moral corruption and pleasure seeking, collapses into chaos and confusion, and finally falls into the hands of an evil dictatorship.

The lesson from biblical history is equally clear. We can learn a profound lesson from Jeremiah. He spoke to the wayward people of Judah just before they were conquered by the Babylonian armies of Nebuchadnezzar. God spoke to the people through Jeremiah and thus communicated two grievances: "My people have committed two evils; [first] they have forsaken me the fountain of living waters, and [second, they have] hewed out cisterns, broken cisterns, that can hold no water" (Jeremiah 2:13).

The nation of Israel had abandoned God's perfect standards and had made up its own rules to the game of life. The result was fatal. Again Jeremiah speaks: "Thou hast forsaken me, saith the LORD, thou art gone backward: therefore will I stretch out my hand against thee, and destroy thee; I am weary with repenting" (Jeremiah 15:6).

Our country has turned its back on God. Will God let us get away with that? The lesson is clear. There are only three paths America can take. First, if she continues her downward moral spiral, she will be conquered either from without or from within. A second possibility is that the Lord Jesus Christ could return at any moment. The only other option is for Christians to change the very destiny of our country and be used of God to usher in a revival the magnitude of which our

What's ahead? Lessons from history and prophecy

America's three choices

country has never seen. It can be done. It must be done. But it will happen only if the church learns to evangelize through multiplication. And that requires a commitment to significant training in evangelism on the part of every Christian. Where do you fit into this great possibility?

HOW TO GAIN MAXIMUM PROFIT FROM THIS MANUAL

It will be tragic if you merely read this material as you would any other book. I urge you to do the following:

First, invite someone who shares your desire to receive training in evangelism to study this material with you. This is critical. All the assignments, memory work, and exercises designed to help you overcome your fears will be pointless if you do not select a workshop partner. Better yet, get together a group of concerned Christians to study this material as a group. A specially prepared leader's guide is available to help you in group study of this book.

Second, consider each chapter a week's assignment. In that way you are not only reading a book, you are enrolled in a course of study of highly condensed material as well. Your course of study will be concluded in thirteen weeks.

Third, say all memory work to your partner, and be hard on each other! Insist that *every* Scripture verse be quoted word perfect.

Fourth, give your written assignments to your partner for a careful critique. Or if you are using this book for group study, have the group leader check each week's assignment.

Fifth, prepare to make your first visit together to share the gospel within two weeks after studying chapter 8. Then continue to make calls together until both of you have had the opportunity to witness at least three times.

Sixth, after you feel comfortable witnessing, both of you determine to teach someone else how to communicate the gospel of grace.

Finally, pray. Right now. Ask the Lord to give you great courage and great responsiveness concerning the lessons in this manual. Meditate on each of the course objectives, which are listed on the next page. Ask the Lord to accomplish each of these objectives in your life during the next exciting weeks.

COURSE OBJECTIVES

1. Developing confidence about and precision in giving your personal testimony

Read these paragraphs carefully

Study with someone!

Do each assignment

Don't neglect the memory work

Stop here . . . pray

26

Your testimony must be condensed into a three-minute time span. Confidence comes with precision. Know where to start and where to conclude, as well as what to say.

2. Learning the three crucial issues in evangelism

   Nothing in our workshop is more important than understanding the three crucial issues clearly. They are to be memorized word perfect.

3. Mastering a strategy for conversation when in homes of unsaved people

   A strategy for conversation is very important. Never omit a time of making the people you are visiting, and yourself, comfortable. Especially crucial is what you say during the first minute of introduction.

4. Knowing a clear outline for presenting the gospel

   Make a complete, workable outline of God's plan of salvation. Then begin to put your personality into this outline.

5. Mastering (memorizing) Scripture verses that deal with each issue in your presentation

   The Holy Spirit convicts and convinces through the Word of God. Learn at least three verses that deal with each point of your outline.

6. Learning to press successfully toward a decision

   It is important to know what the issue is. Many Christians think they have witnessed when they state a religious truth. You have not witnessed until you have confronted a person with his need to place his faith in Christ and asked him to make a decision.

7. Understanding how to answer people's basic questions and objections

   Christians often panic when confronted with an objection. How unfortunate, because we really do have answers to people's basic questions. Let's learn them!

8. Gaining a clear understanding of what issues and clichés are misleading and confusing when presenting the gospel

   We must know how to avoid confusion if we are going to be able to present a message that is the power of God unto salvation.

9. Getting over the "hump" of fear and embarrassment when confronting strangers with the gospel

   This can be done only through actual experience in homes.

REVIEW OF CHAPTER 2
THE NEED FOR EVANGELISM

Someone has said that the church in the twentieth century resembles a professional football game: Seventy thousand spectators desperately in need of exercise watching twenty-two men who are desperately in need of rest.

It is estimated that only four out of every one hundred Christians know how to witness with confidence and precision. How can that be?

1. Church participation has turned into a spectator sport.
    a. Our people will come to church often if the right *Christian celebrity* is giving a sacred concert or if the film has plenty of action.
    b. Gradually, the idea has developed that church attendance is *my service* for Christ rather than *my preparation for service* to Christ every day of the week. This idea could be fatal to the church.
2. What the church was intended to be—a perfect balance between:

EVANGELISM	EDIFICATION	FELLOWSHIP	SERVICE
Going to the lost	Worship	Sharing our lives and the life of Christ with each other	Meeting the needs of people—both Christians and non-Christians
Giving them the gospel where they are	Instruction		
	Prayer	Developing a commonness of concerns	
Bringing them into the fellowship of God's people			

3. What the church often becomes:

EVANGELISM	EDIFICATION	FELLOWSHIP	SERVICE
Supporting a pastor or a minister of education who can reach the lost	Putting on a great show for spectators on Sunday	Enjoying the exclusive company of a few select friends	Putting money into the offering plate

4. The world will never be reached by clergymen.
5. And laymen will not reach the world until:
    a. They realize that they are *every bit as much a minister of Christ, and as responsible for the lost,* as the pastor is.
    b. They are effectively trained in evangelism, so that they will not have to rely on excuses.
    c. They accept the fact that the call to be Christ's disciples is the call to become fishers of men.
    d. They actually see evangelism happen by watching someone in action—someone witnessing.

ASSIGNMENTS

1. It is time to come to grips with yourself about personal evangelism. You have had impulses to get involved in witnessing ever since you were saved. But you have never truly come to grips with the thought of becoming thoroughly trained to tell others about your faith or with building into your life a plan and a time for living an evangelistic life-style. Please, go no further until you weigh this matter carefully. Consider all the past resolutions you have made (dieting, jogging, prayer time, Bible study). How can you put teeth into your attempt to change your witnessing patterns?

    a. Ask God to give you an *evangelism partner*—one who shares your heart and who will not be afraid *to provoke you to good works* (see Hebrews 10:24).

    b. Make a personal commitment—right now—that you will complete each assignment in this manual not somehow, but triumphantly.

    c. Ask the Lord to burden your heart for souls.

    d. Refuse to get upset with the lack of vision of your denomination, church, or friends. (Concentrate only on your needs, your vision, your life.)

    e. Believe that God wants to use you.

2. Learn word perfect the Bible verses on pages 29-31 as they are assigned in the following chapters.

3. Start thinking about how you became a Christian.

QUESTIONS FOR DISCUSSION

1. Why is it so easy—almost natural—for Christians to turn into spectators rather than soldiers?

2. Can anything short of persecution turn our churches around—create an evangelistic zeal in the hearts of Christian laymen?

3. What keeps the people in your church from effectively sharing their faith?

PRAYER

Tell God of your desire to be used. Tell Him that you want your life to count in these amazing days of our world. Be honest and tell God if you have not known much success as a fisher of men. Thank Him for loving you so much in spite of yourself. Tell Him that you long to tell your friends about His love, His grace, and His Son. Tell God that today you commit yourself to the goal of entering into this training with your whole heart. Ask Him to give you the desire to do all things well. Ask Him to turn you into an optimist and make you into a soldier instead of a spectator. Tell God that you count it the joy of your life to know Him. Thank Him for the privilege of being an ambassador of Christ.

SCRIPTURE MEMORY VERSES

1. God is good, a God of love, who does not want anyone to perish.

    John 3:16—For God so loved the world, that he gave his only begotten Son, that whosoever believeth in him should not perish, but have everlasting life.

    1 Timothy 2:4—Who will have all men to be saved, and to come unto the knowledge of the truth.

    2 Peter 3:9—The Lord is not slack concerning his promise, as some men count slackness; but is longsuffering to usward, not willing that any should perish, but that all should come to repentance.

2. But many are perishing. Why? Because all men are sinners.

>   *Isaiah 53:6*—All we like sheep have gone astray; we have turned every one to his own way; and the LORD hath laid on him the iniquity of us all.
>
>   *Jeremiah 17:9*—The heart is deceitful above all things, and desperately wicked: who can know it?
>
>   *Romans 3:10*—As it is written, There is none righteous, no, not one.
>
>   *Romans 3:23*—For all have sinned, and come short of the glory of God.

3. And the penalty of man's sin is death.

>   *Ezekiel 18:4*—The soul that sinneth, it shall die.
>
>   *Romans 6:23*—For the wages of sin is death; but the gift of God is eternal life through Jesus Christ our Lord.
>
>   *Ephesians 2:1*—And you hath he quickened [made alive], who were dead in trespasses and sins.

4. *But Jesus Christ, God's wonderful Son, died on Calvary's cross to pay the full penalty for man's sin.*

>   *Romans 5:8*—But God commendeth his love toward us, in that, while we were yet sinners, Christ died for us.
>
>   *2 Corinthians 5:21*—For he hath made him to be sin for us, who knew no sin; that we might be made the righteousness of God in him.
>
>   *1 Timothy 1:15*—This is a faithful saying, and worthy of all acceptation, that Christ Jesus came into the world to save sinners; of whom I am chief.
>
>   *Hebrews 9:26*—But now once in the end of the world hath he appeared to put away sin by the sacrifice of himself.
>
>   *1 Peter 1:18a, 19*—Forasmuch as ye know that ye were not redeemed with corruptible things, as silver and gold . . . but with the precious blood of Christ, as of a lamb without blemish and without spot.
>
>   *1 Peter 2:24*—Who his own self bare our sins in his own body on the tree, that we, being dead to sins, should live unto righteousness: by whose stripes ye were healed.
>
>   *1 Peter 3:18*—For Christ also hath once suffered for sins, the just for the unjust, that he might bring us to God, being put to death in the flesh, but quickened [made alive] by the Spirit.

5. It is not enough to give mere assent to these truths with the head. Each person must claim by personal choice (will) and rely exclusively upon (trust) Christ's work on the cross to be sufficient payment for his sins.

>   *Romans 3:24-25*—Being justified freely by his grace through the redemption that is in Christ Jesus: whom God hath set forth to be a propitiation through faith in his blood, to declare his righteousness for the remission of sins that are past, through the forbearance of God.
>
>   *Romans 4:20-21*—He staggered not at the promise of God through unbelief; but was strong in faith, giving glory to God; and being fully persuaded that, what he had promised, he was able also to perform.
>
>   *Hebrews 6:18*—We . . . have a strong consolation, who have fled for refuge to lay hold upon the hope set before us.

Verses of Decision:

>   *John 1:12*—But as many as received him, to them gave he power to become the sons of God, even to them that believe on his name.
>
>   *John 6:37*—All that the Father giveth me shall come to me; and him that cometh to me I will in no wise cast out.

Romans 10:9-10—That if thou shalt confess with thy mouth the Lord Jesus, and shalt believe in thine heart that God hath raised him from the dead, thou shalt be saved. For with the heart man believeth unto righteousness; and with the mouth confession is made unto salvation.

Verses on assurance:

John 3:36—He that believeth on the Son hath everlasting life: and he that believeth not the Son shall not see life; but the wrath of God abideth on him.

John 5:24—Verily, verily, I say unto you, He that heareth my word, and believeth on him that sent me, hath everlasting life, and shall not come into condemnation; but is passed from death unto life.

John 6:47—Verily, verily, I say unto you, He that believeth on me hath everlasting life.

Romans 5:1—Therefore being justified by faith, we have peace with God through our Lord Jesus Christ.

1 John 5:11-13a—And this is the record, that God hath given to us eternal life, and this life is in his Son. He that hath the Son hath life; and he that hath not the Son of God hath not life. These things have I written unto you that believe on the name of the Son of God; that ye may know that ye have eternal life.

Verses that prove that salvation is by faith alone, and not by works:

Romans 4:5—But to him that worketh not, but believeth on him that justifieth the ungodly, his faith is counted for righteousness.

Galatians 2:21—I do not frustrate [make void] the grace of God: for if righteousness come by the law then Christ is dead in vain.

Ephesians 2:8-9—For by grace are ye saved through faith; and that not of yourselves: it is the gift of God: not of works, lest any man should boast.

Titus 3:5-6—Not by works of righteousness which we have done, but according to his mercy he saved us, by the washing of regeneration, and renewing of the Holy Ghost; which he shed on us abundantly through Jesus Christ our Saviour.

3

Overcoming Our Fears

PASTOR'S DILEMMA

**Is witnessing
pleasurable or
terrifying?**

Pastors who are concerned about training laymen to evangelize face a dilemma. As they describe the work of evangelism, should they depict it as being pleasurable or frightening? Is evangelism fun or fearful? Is it natural to share your faith, or does it require energy and effort?

If a pastor were to say, "Sharing your faith is the most exciting and pleasurable experience in life—if you are looking for pleasure, come and help us change the world," many people would not respond. They would conclude that if the pursuit of excitement and pleasure leads people into witnessing, they have just about all the pleasure they can handle. They feel that they can find joy in other ways. Besides, there is not much about witnessing to make it look pleasurable.

Another pastor says, "Sharing your faith is to be seen as a sobering responsibility. It is nothing but hard work. It is part of bearing the reproach of Christ. It is anything but pleasurable." People fail to respond because they get the impression that witnessing is such a drudgery that the only way anyone gets involved is if he has had his arm twisted.

Do you see the dilemma? If we say that sharing Christ is pleasurable, we run the risk of excusing those who don't see any fun in it at all. But if we affirm that evangelism is an arduous task, we run the risk of failing to capture the imagination of those who believe that telling others about the gospel of Christ ought to be the most thrilling experience in the world.

The solution to the dilemma is to affirm that evangelism is an *exciting responsibility*. It is both pleasurable and difficult. Sharing Christ is both a privilege and an obligation. Someone has said that the difference between children and adults is that children do what they want to do and adults do what they have to do. Obviously, that is not completely true. The happiest and most mature people are those who like to do what they have to do.

Much of evangelism is never pleasurable. A man has to have a morbid outlook on life to enjoy the sensation of telling other men they are lost, hell-deserving sinners. It is never fun to make yourself vulnerable. It is not easy to intrude into another family's life and home or ring a stranger's doorbell with the hope of sharing your faith. What kind of person thrives on the feeling that men think he is strange, weird, or fanatical? Who among us enjoys encountering people's objections to the gospel message? Evangelism is difficult because it involves the fear of all those things. And fear is no easy thing to overcome.

There are aspects of evangelism that are not pleasurable—we must be constrained by Christ's love

Note, however, that much in evangelism is exceedingly pleasurable. Joy is the product of accomplishment. There is great satisfaction in a job well done. There is excitement in knowing that you are a soldier of Jesus Christ. The thrill of seeing someone place his trust in Christ is nothing short of spectacular. Adrenalin begins to flow at the thought of telling someone the truth of the gospel and at the thought that the destiny of an eternal soul may be changed forever.

But there is great joy as well

If we do not learn how to overcome our fears, we will never be able to experience the joy and satisfaction that are by-products of witnessing. That is a serious issue. During the course of this week, will you take a few hours to analyze your fears? Just what scares you about sharing your faith? Here are some possibilities:

1. The fear of rejection
2. The fear of ridicule
3. The fear of failure
4. The fear of bodily injury
5. The fear of hypocrisy
6. The fear of not knowing what to say
7. The fear of not knowing how a person will respond
8. The fear of trying something new and unfamiliar
9. The fear of not being smart enough to answer objections

Circle the fears with which you clearly identify

10. The fear of intruding into the private areas of people's lives
11. The fear of the unknown
12. The fear of past experiences in witnessing
13. The fear that your fears will show
14. The fear that the gospel will not be effective in this situation
15. The fear that you are not worthy to share this great message
16. The fear that you will say something wrong

THE NATURE OF FEAR

Fear is reasonable—all Christians face it

Of these and many other kinds of fears, several conclusions can be drawn. First, *fear is rational*. An irrational fear is called a phobia. It is almost impossible to convince a person with a phobia that there is nothing to worry about. But fear does have a rational base. Let's face it—any of the fears on the above list just might be realized. Saints of past ages have given their lives for their faith.

In the book of Acts, five thousand people gathered in wonder after a lame man was healed. The magistrates asked how such a miracle could happen. Peter announced that this miracle was accomplished by the power of the risen Christ. He proceeded to add that Christ is not only a miracle worker, but the only hope of sinful men as well. "Neither is there salvation in any other: for there is none other name under heaven given among men, whereby we must be saved" (Acts 4:12). Peter made that statement after spending the night in prison—and he said it to those who had crucified Christ for saying the same thing. The magistrates threatened Peter and John, forbidding them to speak the name of Jesus Christ. Do you remember their noble response? "We cannot but speak of the things which we have seen and heard" (Acts 4:20). Later, when the apostles were released, they returned to their brethren and decided to have a prayer meeting. Unlike some of us who would have prayed, "Lord, deliver us from this mess," they said, "Lord, behold their threatenings: and grant unto thy servants, that with all boldness they may speak thy word" (Acts 4:29).

The disciples could have been overcome by rational fear

Had they looked at the situation humanistically, they would *reasonably* have been terrified. But these rational men with rational fears also had rational reasons not to panic. They knew that

34

God was in this thing. Here is the secret: Men cannot have faith in God and be overcome with fear at the same time. Jesus said: "Let not your heart be troubled: ye believe in God, believe also in me" (John 14:1). You cannot be troubled and be believing at the same time. Here is God's promise: "Let your conversation [manner of life] be without covetousness; and be content with such things as ye have: for he hath said, I will never leave thee, nor forsake thee. So that we may boldly say, the Lord is my helper, and I will not fear what man shall do unto me" (Hebrews 13:5-6).

Just as *fear is rational,* so is faith. Faith in God is reasonable, if He is the God He claims to be. When we know the workings of God, we find excitement in proving God, taking risks, and making ourselves vulnerable for His sake.

We can cope with our fear, because we have faith in the power of God. If your fears have so paralyzed you that you take no risks in your daily service for Christ, *your life is boring.* If your life is not a successive demonstration that our God is a supernatural God, your life is dull.

Second, *fear is sin.* That is, it becomes sin if it keeps you from doing God's will. God has given us the power to overcome all our fears. That is why Paul could tell Timothy, "God hath not given us the Spirit of fear: but of power, and of love, and of a sound mind" (2 Timothy 1:7). It is a slap in God's face to tell Him you cannot do what He empowers you to do. Christ said, "All power is given unto me. Go ye therefore, and teach all nations . . . I am with you alway" (Matthew 28:18-20).

Third, *fear is constant.* That is somewhat difficult to explain. Let me try by using the flesh as an illustration. The Bible describes our flesh as a subconscious impulse to sin that never leaves us. That impulse in itself is not sin until one consciously chooses to sin. The flesh is constantly there, but its impulse by itself is not sin.

It is folly to expect the Lord to take our wrong desires away. That isn't going to happen. God did not make us that way. Flesh is a constant. We don't give up sweets because God has taken the taste away. We give them up because we have stronger impulses that now motivate us to think about our health and to want to be suitable ambassadors for Christ.

Perhaps I use that illustration because it hits so close to home. I have been fighting the battle of

Instead, they overcame fear through faith in a God who is real

Fear is sin if it renders you powerless

Fear is a constant, because it is part of the flesh—you don't get rid of it; you overcome it

the bulge all my life. But if I wait to give up ice cream until I have no taste for ice cream, I will never stop eating it. And if I can, with greater impulses, overcome my impulse to eat sweets, I'll win.

It is precisely the same with fears about sharing Christ. If you make a deal with God and tell Him that as soon as He takes away all your fear you will begin to share your faith, that day will never come. We are not immobilized because we have fears, but because we haven't learned how to overcome those fears with greater impulses.

IMPULSES THAT CAN OVERCOME FEAR

What are some of those impulses that can help us overcome our fear of witnessing? There are several.

1. First is *the love of Christ.* The most stunning of all realities is that Christ loved me enough to die for me. His love melts hearts. It changes lives. But it also causes one to come to some important conclusions: "For the love of Christ constraineth [compels] us; because we thus judge, that if one died for all, then were all dead: and that He died for all, that they which live should not henceforth live unto themselves, but unto him which died for them, and rose again" (2 Corinthians 5:14-15).

It is a wonderful thing to know the love of God. The pleasure of the realization that God loves you is sweet indeed. Then comes that traumatic moment when you discover the truth of 2 Corinthians 5:14-15. You discover that God feels the same way about others as He feels about you. And apart from Christ they are *all dead.* But God does not want anyone to perish. He commissions all those who know Him to become His instruments for reaching a doomed planet. You are confronted with this question: Will I live for myself, or will I live for Him? We all want somehow to answer "Myself!" But the love of Christ compels us to answer "Him!" That is not law; it is pure grace.

But the power of His love has a wonderful effect on our fears. John declares, "There is no fear in love; but perfect love casteth out fear" (1 John 4:18).

While Christ walked this earth, especially in the latter days, He had much to fear. Yet He set His face toward Jerusalem. Luke reveals the inner turmoil of Christ when he quotes the Savior: "I have a baptism to be baptized with; and how I am

Love can compel us to do things that don't come naturally

What do these verses teach?

The constraint of Christ to go to Jerusalem

36

straitened till it be accomplished" (Luke 12:50).
What was His baptism? The parallel passage in
Matthew 20:18-19 makes it clear: "Behold, we go
up to Jerusalem; and the Son of man shall be
betrayed unto the chief priests and unto the
scribes, and they shall condemn him to death,
and shall deliver him to the Gentiles to mock, and
to scourge, and to crucify him. And the third day
he shall rise again."

Clearly, our Lord was compelled to do something that did not come naturally. Every man naturally fights for his life. The love of Christ makes
us willing to give it away. A missionary was
warned not to leave the ship to take his post in a
South Sea island because the natives were canni-
bals. The ship's crew warned him, "If you go to
that island you will die." His saintly response was,
"I died before I came here!" He was compelled
by the love of Christ.

I believe God is at work in your life. If it were
not so you would have no interest in this book.
You are aware that God loves men in Africa and
China and Cincinnati just as much as He loves
you. You know that God is vitally concerned
about your relatives, friends, and acquaintances
at work. He is at work within you to win these
people with the message of eternal life. You will
find that if you open your heart to God, His concerns will become yours. His passions will be your
passions. His loves your loves. And his love will
overshadow your fear.

2. A second impulse that can overcome fear in
witnessing is *the setting apart of your life for the
Lord.* In order to understand this issue, we must
hear the words of Peter: "Sanctify the Lord God
in your hearts: and be ready always to give an
answer to every man that asketh you a reason of
the hope that is in you with meekness and fear"
(1 Peter 3:15). If you are not ready always, you
will be ready never. You must come to the point in
your life where you can say: "Lord, my life today
is in Your hands. I regard the use of its precious
moments as a divine stewardship. Direct my path
to a thirsty soul. I live today for the opportunity to
make Christ known." Otherwise, you will probably be one of those typical Christians who never
seem to have a witnessing opportunity.

Peter is saying that there is a state of mind that
readies a man to talk to others about Christ. That
state of mind manifests itself in at least four ways.
First, there is a conscious setting apart of one's life
for divine purposes. That is what *sanctification*

**Set your life apart
for spiritual
purposes—it is a
key in discovering
witnessing
opportunities**

**You will "be
ready" always . . .
or never!**

**The way to "be
ready":**

**1. Your life . . . the
Lord's**

37

2. A sense of expectation

3. Data to be mastered

4. Dependence on God

Peter knew that he had the medicine

means. Second, there is an expectation that an opportunity awaits. It has been said that there are three kinds of people. There are those who make opportunities happen, those who take advantage of ready-made opportunities, and those who would not recognize an opportunity if they were hit in the head with one. Third, there is an awareness that data are to be mastered. Believers are to have answers. Indeed, they are to have answers at their fingertips. People are lost and seeking answers, and it is our responsibility to have those answers and know how to communicate them. Fourth, there is an attitude of heart that depends on God. It is dangerous to get cocky about evangelism. There are mysteries here. This is God's business. We cannot depend on Madison Avenue techniques to win souls. Every person is gloriously unique. Evangelism is a place for meekness and fear.

As we set apart our lives for the Lord, we have made a powerful advance in the war against our fears. It's time for you to evaluate precisely where you are. Do you really want victory over fear in witnessing? Then set apart the Lord in your heart by saying "I am living today for Christ."

3. A third impulse that can overcome fear in witnessing is *confidence in our medicine*. In Acts 3 we see the first miracle performed by the apostles in the name of the resurrected Savior. A lame man is begging at the Temple gate. Peter and John see him. They stop and say: "Look on us." His eyes brighten with anticipation. Will he receive a nickel or a quarter? Then comes Peter's sublime words: "Silver and gold have I none; but such as I have give I thee: In the name of Jesus Christ of Nazareth rise up and walk" (Acts 3:4-6). Peter was absolutely confident in the power of God's Word. He knew it would met the need perfectly.

When I was a student in college I was a brand new Christian. At that time I had no confidence in my medicine. When I would make a feeble attempt at witnessing, it would sound something like this: "Oh, pardon me, I know you are a very well adjusted person whose life is wonderfully integrated and satisfying, but I wonder if you would do me a favor and listen to me for five minutes as I share with you some remote facts that you probably don't need or desire to hear about, but I sure would appreciate it if you would do me a favor and listen, and if you do I promise I will go away and stop bothering you, and never trouble you again!"

38

Is there any wonder why I did not win many people to Christ? I was living in a bubble, expecting it to burst at any moment. But I have changed since then, and so has the world. The complacent 50s are gone forever. Our world is in despair. It needs a doctor. It is sick and dying. And I have the only medicine that can cure it.

Some patients in mental hospitals think that their doctors are sick. And it is true that some people think I am a religious fanatic. But *never again will I lose sight of who is the doctor and who is the patient.* No one is doing me a favor by listening. No matter how calm the exterior of men's lives, I know that they are fighting battles. It has changed my entire ministry to be aware of the truth that I have something wonderful for people. I have medicine that works. All other remedies are poisonous. When we see what we have to offer to a sick society, we have new confidence.

4. Another impulse that can overcome fear is *the joy of being obedient to the great order of our Commander.* The Scriptures frequently use the metaphor of a soldier. For example, Paul says, "No man that warreth entangleth himself with the affairs of this life; that he may please him who hath chosen him to be a soldier" (2 Timothy 2:4). We are soldiers of Christ. The Lord Jesus Christ is our Captain. He has given us one great command. "Go ye therefore, and teach all nations, baptizing them in the name of the Father, and of the Son, and of the Holy Ghost: teaching them to observe all things whatsoever I have commanded you: and, lo, I am with you alway, even unto the end of the world" (Matthew 28:19-20).

Often I feel that the greatest joy of life results simply from the consciousness that you are doing what is right. There is sublime peace in the confidence that you are doing the will of God. That is why a ditchdigger or a mechanic or a machine operator can have joy in his work. He is not working for men; he is working for God.

If there is some doubt about the specifics of the life that pleases God, there can be little doubt about the basics. God desires that the life of His Son be seen in us. Moreover, His plan from eternity is that we become His channels through which the life of Christ can change the lives of a lost world. When we teach the gospel and a person receives Christ as Savior, it is as though a little voice inside says, "Mission accomplished!" In fact, as the small teams of young evangelists go out from our church each Tuesday night, there is a

In spite of appearances, all are fighting inner battles

Great joy comes from obedience

A lesson to those who lack "ego strength"

great feeling of accomplishment and satisfaction, even if no one is saved. That feeling of joy from obedience is a great weapon against the fear of witnessing.

5. Another aid in overcoming fear is *the ability to distinguish between personal rejection and the rejection of our message.* I'll never forget the first time a door was slammed in my face. It was a totally humiliating experience. I was taking part in a neighborhood canvass during my seminary years. I went up to the door with a big smile on my face, and when a middle-aged man came to the door, I said, "Hello, I'm Dick Sisson from Meadows Baptist Church. We are a friendly church committed to the twin beliefs that the Bible is the Word of God and that Jesus Christ died to be our Savior!"

Slam! The door vibrated from the force of a powerful man's anger.

Thinking back over that experience, I recall that as I walked away I asked myself (in the typical insecure fashion of today's young people): "Why didn't he like me?" Soon it became obvious: he didn't even know me. We had never before met. That closed door did not represent his attitude toward my personality, my sociability, my appearance, or my friendliness. He was upset because I had named the name of Christ.

Some of the Savior's last words to His disciples were, "Remember the word that I said unto you, The servant is not greater than his lord. If they have persecuted me, they will also persecute you . . . but all these things will they do unto you for my name's sake" (John 15:20-21). I had learned an important lesson. It is often my *message,* not my *personality,* that offends. Now, as a minister of the gospel, I see this phenomenon repeated many times over. As I introduce myself in certain situations, I become aware of an instant coolness. I'm so glad I learned early how to cope with the psychological defense-mechanism of projection. People project their attitudes toward Christ onto me, His representative. What a great honor it is to stand in the stead of Christ.

Consider the words of Jeremiah: "Oh, Lord, thou knowest: remember me, and visit me, and revenge me of my persecutors; take me not away in thy long-suffering: know that for thy sake I have suffered rebuke. Thy words were found, and I did eat them; and thy word was unto me the joy and rejoicing of mine heart: for I am called by thy

40

name, O LORD God of hosts" (Jeremiah 15:15-16).

6. A final impulse that will aid in overcoming fear is an understanding of *the condition of our present world.* Let me make a prediction. If the world continues to turn its back on God and things become worse and worse, Christians will begin to wake up to the realization that the fears that accompany the presenting of the gospel will look pale by comparison to the fears we all will know if the message of Christ is not presented. The issue seems clear. Christ is the only one who can save our country from self-destruction. Picture absolutely amoral packs of teenagers rampaging through our streets unchecked. It could happen. Our schools could become chambers of horror, our courts and police forces a mockery.

Christians are the salt of the earth. If they fail to represent Christ, our world will decay into frightful corruption before our eyes. People will have no inhibitions. They will demonstrate the vile behavior patterns that other generations have succeeded in suppressing.

I have three young children. I want more for them than that. When I consider that I can have a part in shaping the destiny of the world in which my children will live, my fears about evangelism seem trivial. When the issue is survival, fears about reputation and ruffling people's feathers become an unaffordable luxury.

Time is running out. It makes no difference if you are an environmentalist, a politician, a census taker, a sociologist, or a prophet. The handwriting is on the wall. What we intend to do for the cause of Christ and His Kingdom, we had better do now. This is not the time to keep our talents in reserve and our money in the bank. It has often been said, "We shall have all eternity to enjoy our crowns, but only a few short hours in which to win them."

THREE IMPORTANT POSTSCRIPTS CONCERNING FEAR

I want to conclude this chapter with three postscripts about our fears. *First,* we need soberly to remind ourselves that *sin robs us of courage.* This happens in two ways: we lose our moral backbone, and we become preoccupied with our own guilt feelings. God told Isaiah, "Fear thou not; for I am with thee . . . yea, I will uphold thee with the right hand of my righteousness" (Isaiah 41:10). There is strength in righteousness. When

Are you afraid? If we fail to evangelize, we'll really have reason to fear

Sin robs us of courage

41

we know that we are walking in the light, we are confident.

Military personnel tell us that morale is the great intangible determiner of victory. When an army is corrupt and its cause is not just, its men will not fight to win. History records what a few men are capable of doing when they are committed to the rightness of their task. Paul told Timothy, "God sent you out to battle for the right, armed only with your faith and a clear conscience" (1 Timothy 1:19, Phillips).*

Christian, if you are playing around with sin, you will never succeed in evangelism. You will be overcome with your fears and preoccupied with your own guilt. You will become introspective, never able to get your eyes off yourself to see that there are fields white unto harvest.

The *second* postscript is most important. Remember *every* time you approach a stranger's door that after you state your purpose *the person to whom you are speaking will probably be more afraid of you than you are of him.* The full impact of that truth hit me last summer when I determined to use my Saturday mornings to ring door bells in our neighborhood on a block-to-block basis. I noticed that people often stood quivering as I shared that I was a Christian and bound for heaven. My heart went out to each of them. I felt like patting them on the back and saying, "It's all right! It's only me. Don't be afraid. I just stopped by to tell you something wonderful!"

The next time you pity yourself for the fears you feel as you approach a stranger's door, take a moment to pity the poor person who must open the door and meet, perhaps for the first time in his life, a Christian with a big smile on his face who knows that he is going to heaven.

Finally, remember that *the ultimate answer to the question of fear is simply facing the thing that you fear most.* People are terrified when they visit homes of strangers. Yet, with each passing week and each new exposure to the situation they fear, that anxiety is reduced. I know I speak for many of our trainers when I say that they no longer even think about fear as they prepare themselves to train people on Tuesday nights. What has made the difference? They have faced their fear honestly, and through constant exposure to the thing that causes them their anxieties they develop the ability to gain personal victory.

The people to whom you are talking about your faith will also be afraid

We simply must face that which we fear

New Testament in Modern English (Phillips)

42

REVIEW OF CHAPTER 3
OVERCOMING OUR FEARS

1. Fear is a constant.

   As with our flesh (another constant), we are not to try to eliminate our fears, but rather to *overcome them* by being motivated by *stronger impulses.*

2. Scripture details the stronger impulses that should overcome our fears.

   a. *The love of Christ* (2 Corinthians 5:14-15).

      These are two of the most profound verses in the Bible. First there is the love of Christ *for* me (Calvary), and now there is the love of Christ *in* me because I have the mind of Christ (Philippians 2:5). As we realize this impulse better and understand our wonderful Savior's burden, the urge to tell others the gospel of grace becomes literally irresistible.

   b. *The setting apart of your life for spiritual pursuits* (1 Peter 3:15).

      The key to being "ready always" is the knowledge that I have come to the point in my life where I can honestly say, "I live for Christ." The word "sanctify" literally means "set Christ apart decisively as the great purpose in your life."

   c. *Confidence in your "medicine"* (Acts 3: 4-6).

      Too many Christians apologize for their Christianity. You will never help anyone unless you are persuaded that that person you are afraid to talk to is desperately *sick* (not you!) and that you are the *doctor* (not the patient) with the right *medicine* (the message).

   d. *The joy of simply being obedient to the great order of our commander* (Matthew 28:19-20).

   e. *An ability to distinguish between personal rejection and the rejection of your message.*

      Remember, it is your *message,* not your personality, that offends.

   f. *The condition of our present world.*

3. Three important postscripts concerning fear.

   a. Remember that *sin robs us of courage.*

      You can easily become so preoccupied with *your guilt* that you don't even expect anyone to respect your message.

   b. The people you talk to are more afraid of you than you are of them.

   c. Face your fear honestly, but keep witnessing.

ASSIGNMENTS

1. Memorize word-perfect the following verses:
   a. John 3:16   b. 1 Timothy 2:4   c. 2 Peter 3:9
   Quote those verses to your evangelism partner next week.
2. List fears that you know keep you from presenting Christ effectively.

3. Review carefully six ways we overcome our fears.

QUESTIONS FOR DISCUSSION

1. Why do we suggest that fear is a constant?
2. What part has fear played in your own life in keeping you from witnessing?
3. Why do we suggest that fear is sin?
4. Discuss carefully the meaning of 2 Corinthians 5:14-15.
5. Have you ever consciously set apart your life for spiritual pursuits?
6. Make a list of at least five reasons a Christian can have confidence in his medicine.
7. How does sin rob us of courage?

PRAYER

Pray that none of the fears listed in this chapter will rob you of the exciting challenge of witnessing.

4

Mastering the Three Crucial Issues

If fear is the primary obstacle to overcome in order to witness, uncertainty about precisely what the gospel is certainly follows close behind. Think about it. Paul reminded Timothy that the body of truths that make up the gospel is precious. Indeed, it is the most precious message in the world. Paul said, "That good thing [that precious deposit] which was committed unto thee keep by the Holy Ghost which dwelleth in us" (2 Timothy 1:14). Paul's frame of mind comes through unmistakably: "Timothy, you must guard with your life this sacred message that can save men's souls."

The gospel is not only precious. It is precise. There is a point beyond which we do not go in attempting to simplify the gospel. But all of us need to see the basic issues of the gospel so clearly that telling them to others becomes second nature. When the eyes of our understanding become enlightened, we will become uncompromisingly jealous about how Christ is presented to people.

The next few pages are critical. They deal with the three most important issues in life. For maximum benefit I urge you to read this chapter through at one sitting. Then memorize the three great issues in evangelism *word perfect*. Finally, reread the chapter several more times, noting carefully the subtle implications of each of the great issues.

If you do that, you will never again be confused about what a person needs to know in order to pass from death to life. In future chapters we will be concentrating on *how* to share these truths. In this chapter we are concerned only that you understand *what* the issues are. When you understand, you will be horrified to realize that so much

The gospel is not vague

Memorize the three crucial issues

45

of what you hear from people who think they are witnessing is not the gospel at all.

I stress these things because so many contemporary Christians are confused about the plan of salvation. We must recapture the excitement of believing that the gospel is objective. It is not mystical. We do not offer men a vague Christ. We offer them a sure hope. Ours is not a religion of unidentifiable vibrations; it is based on rational, eternal propositions that God tells us simply to believe.

Here, then, is the bedrock of the gospel. It can be reduced no further. Master these three concepts and you are well on your way to being a vibrant witness.

MAN'S PROBLEM—
ALL MEN ARE SINNERS,
AND SIN SEPARATES US FROM GOD

ALL ARE SINNERS

To master this first issue we must know what sin is. There is much confusion about it. Recently I spoke to one of my relatives about Christ. I told her that all men are sinners.

Her response was immediate. "Oh, I'm not a sinner!" She was absolutely sincere. To her, sin meant being indicted for a felony. Sinners were locked behind bars. The world was made up of basically good people and basically bad people, and she was one of the former. Sin is something that a good person would never dream of doing, something like killing or committing armed robbery or aggravated assault.

Not so, according to Scripture. There, we discover that sin is not so much a matter of what we do, it is a matter of who we are. And just what is the biblical description of the natural state of man apart from Christ? The Bible says, "All we like sheep have gone astray; we have turned every one to his own way; and the LORD hath laid on Him the iniquity of us all" (Isaiah 53:6).

Let's use that verse as a jumping off point in our search for the real issues in defining sin. The phrase "his own way" arrests our attention. That is precisely what twentieth-century man is seeking—his own way. This is the fundamental flaw in humanity. It is why sparks fly when one human being is with another for any length of time. In light of that, I want to suggest three truths about sin.

1. Sin is living a life that is enslaved to the *me first* impulse.

The gospel has a fixed base—there is a limit to how far it can be reduced

Sin—a matter of what we are

Living by the *me first* principle

46

2. The *me first* impulse forces us into conscious rebellion against God.

3. Outward sins are merely the fruit of a selfish life.

Sin, therefore, can be defined in three ways. It is

1. Demanding our own way (autonomy),

2. Defying the will of God (rebellion), or

3. Being driven by selfishness to do wrong things (unrighteousness).

DEMANDING OUR OWN WAY

There are many differences between people today. People are rich, poor, backward, progressive, Communist, or capitalist. But all people share one trait—they want their own way. They all live by the *me first* impulse. Labor unions want their way, big business wants its way; professional athletes want astronomical salaries, owners want to be able to control their athletic teams; parents want kids to obey, teenagers rebel. Try to find someone who will give you a break in a traffic jam. Lobbyists in Washington are fighting for their own interests. Everyone seems to look out only for himself.

Most people will confess that they don't look at that attitude as sin. But rest assured that they will identify personally with *every* word.

DEFYING THE WILL OF GOD

When we extend the *me first* principle Godward, we are talking about rebellion. Romans devastatingly and clearly describes how selfish men handle the knowledge of God: "Even as they did not like to retain God in their knowledge, God gave them over to a reprobate mind" (Romans 1:28).

Men are sharp in disguising their rebellion. One radio announcer, just before he signs off each Saturday night, says, "Good night folks, and don't forget to give an hour to the good Lord tomorrow." What he is really saying—and what millions of religious people say—is, "Lord, I'll make a deal with you. I'll give you an hour of my time on Sunday—but *the rest of the week is my own*." Do you know people who feel that way?

An hour on Sunday

Today not only individuals but nations as well are determined to root out all God-consciousness from their societies. Courts attack public prayer, the FCC regulates Christian broadcasting, and Christian teachers run the risk of losing their jobs if they mention their faith in Christ.

"God, stay out of my life!"

It is the unrelenting cry of the subconscious, *God, stay out of my life. I want to do it my way. I can be happier if I plan my life. Just leave me alone. I'm doing fine all by myself. I pay my debt to you every Sunday. But it's my life. No one is going to tell me what to do. From now on, it's me first.*

BEING DRIVEN BY SELFISHNESS TO DO WRONG THINGS

The seeds of spiritual rebellion always produce visible fruit. Eventually, what we think about affects what we do. Satan is masterful at exploiting our selfish impulse. Paul told Titus, "We ourselves also were sometimes foolish, disobedient, deceived, serving divers lusts and pleasures" (Titus 3:3). Let's work backward on that statement. Paul describes the *me first* impulse with the words "serving divers [various] lusts and pleasures." Satan knows our hearts. He deceives us by making us think that if we disobey God we will be happy. We succumb. Yet instead of being happy we are plagued with guilt and frustration. We have been deceived into disobeying God, and Satan laughs because he has made us fools.

We are not sinners because we sin; we sin because we are sinners

James gives further insight into the process by which selfish impulses grow into sinful acts. "Every man is tempted, when he is drawn away of his own lust, and enticed. Then when lust hath conceived, it bringeth forth sin: and sin, when it is finished, bringeth forth death" (James 1:14-15). The sequence is deception, desire, disobedience, and death. Satan can persuade men to act sinfully because they think sinfully. We are not sinners because we sin: we sin because we are sinners.

SIN SEPARATES US FROM GOD

The definition of death is separation

Sin separates us from God. *Separation* is the perfect one-word definition of death. My children ask, "Daddy, what happens when you die?" I respond that a separation has taken place.

Remember Adam and Eve?

Let's go back to the beginning of the Bible to see how death is separation. Adam and Eve were enjoying a rich, living experience of communion with God. Their fellowship, however, was rooted in an agreement. "The LORD God commanded the man, saying, Of every tree of the garden thou mayest freely eat: but of the tree of the knowledge of good and evil, thou shalt not eat of it; for in the day that thou eatest thereof thou shalt surely die" (Genesis 2:16-18).

Eve was deceived, and Adam was disobedient.

48

They ate the fruit, but they continued their existence. How could that be? God had decreed that in the very same day that they tasted the fruit, they would die. The answer is that they did die. They began to disintegrate physically (which eventually resulted in their physical deaths), and they immediately died spiritually. That is, they felt strange in God's presence, so they ran from Him. Fellowship was broken. Separation had begun. They were dead. They were forced by sin to leave te Garden of Eden. They were banished—separated—from God's presence.

Death is God's irrevocable judgment upon sin. Sin always brings death. In the Bible, death is pictured in three ways.

Three kinds of death:

1. It is physical death, the separation of body and soul.

1. Separation of body from soul

2. It is spiritual death, the separation of God's Spirit from my spirit.

3. It is the second death, or separation from God forever in hell.

PHYSICAL DEATH

Every human being (except those who live to see the Lord return) will one day die. When a person dies, his heart stops beating. But that is not really the key to understanding death. Not only does the heart stop beating, but the person's soul is separated from the body as well. That soul will never die. The Scripture teaches, "It is appointed unto men once to die, but after this the judgment" (Hebrews 9:27).

SPIRITUAL DEATH

2. Separation of my life from God's life

The Bible says that until I became a partaker of new life in Christ, I was spiritually dead. "And you hath he quickened [made alive], who were dead in trespasses and sins" (Ephesians 2:1). You say, "Who me? Dead? Why, I just ran five miles! I have a strong pulse, and my body temperature is ninety-eight point six. Dead?" Yes, dead. Of course, I am not speaking of physical death now, but spiritual death. When my life is separated from the life of God, I am spiritually dead.

Perhaps you can see that what I am saying is not so far-fetched after all. Have you ever walked through the streets of a large city? If you have, you have noticed thousands of people who have the look of death. Their faces tell the story. They have no joy, no purpose, no hope. They are dead. They are aliens. People go insane when they are without purpose, without love, without God.

49

They become enraged and violent. That is precisely what is happening in America.

THE SECOND DEATH

Yet another kind of death is what the Bible calls "the second death" (Revelation 21:8). It is separation from the life of God forever in hell. The writer of the book of Revelation speaks of the second death; "And death and hell were cast into the lake of fire. This is the second death. And whosoever was not found written in the book of life was cast into the lake of fire" (Revelation 20:14-15).

3. Separation from God forever

GOD'S SOLUTION— CALVARY IS GOD'S ONLY PROVISION FOR MAN'S SIN

If we have been sharing some sobering thoughts up to this point, we now come to the most glorious announcement that human ears have ever heard. Good news! God has taken the initiative in dealing with sin. He sent His Son, Jesus Christ, to die for our sins on the cross of Calvary. Let's look closely at the implications of this second great issue in evangelism.

The good news—Calvary

WE ARE NOT SAVED BY OUR PERFORMANCE, WE ARE SAVED BY HIS SACRIFICE

There is a truth that the natural man cannot grasp without the illumination of the Holy Spirit, and it is that he can do nothing meritorious that will commend him to God. Men would like to believe that the solution to their spiritual need is within their power to implement. Human beings have all kinds of human solutions for their sin problems: baptism, good works, confirmation exercises, church attendance, confessions, sacraments, tithes, service, communion, faithfulness, turning over a new leaf, vows, promises, resolutions, new beginnings, keeping the Golden Rule, living by the Ten Commandments, positive thinking, feelings, religious experiences, and speaking in tongues. God has just one solution—Calvary. Calvary is God's only provision for man's sin.

The human way of salvation is always a matter of performance

We live in a performance-oriented society. If we do something nice for Joe, Joe will do something nice for us. No one gets something for nothing. No one loves for nothing. Ulterior motives lurk behind acts of kindness and charity. As a pastor, I am amazed at the way people perceive the salvation experience. Most of them are trying to think of a way that they can get God to accept them. If they can just give up smoking, or stop cursing, or begin to live like a Christian, then God perhaps will accept them. But that is totally wrong. God does not ask anything from my flesh. He wants me to see that I am bankrupt. I have nothing to offer Him.

The issue is not whether God will accept me; the issue is whether I will accept God's perfect provision for my sin. God doesn't want my performance. He wants my faith in His Son's performance. Peter says: "Forasmuch as ye know that ye were not redeemed with corruptible things, as silver and gold . . . but with the precious blood of Christ, as of a lamb without blemish and without spot" (1 Peter 1:18-19). It is my faith in Christ's work that brings lasting peace to my heart. Nothing else can.

CALVARY: THE ONLY PROVISION

There are many today who say, "I believe that Jesus Christ died on the cross." Yet they have no peace. Think of all the sincere people who attend masses and religious services that depict the suffering of the Lord Jesus. They know the various stations of the cross, they know His last words, they know what happened in the upper room and in the Garden of Gethsemane. Yet they have no peace.

Peace will elude everyone who denies that Christ paid the total cost of redemption. There is something in the unregenerate mind that wants to add something—anything—to Christ's work. Salvation seems so much more reasonable if we can earn it some way. But God is jealous of His Son's blood. The Bible says: "I do not frustrate the grace of God: for if righteousness come by the law, then Christ is dead in vain" (Galations 2:21). Calvary is God's only provision for man's sin. When we try to add human performance to grace, we pollute grace. We are saved either by what we do or by what He did. Take your choice. Listen carefully to the words of the apostle Paul: "If by grace, then it is no more of works: otherwise grace is no more grace. But if it be of works, then it is no more grace: otherwise work is no more work" (Romans 11:6).

Here is the sobering test. I know a woman who is kindly and sincere. She says she believes that Jesus Christ was inspired. She calls herself a Christian and never misses a Sunday in church. But she thinks that all people, even if they *depend* on sacraments, on baptisms, or on living by the Ten Commandments for salvation, as long as they

The issue: Will I accept God's perfect provision?

The cross—it must be the exclusive object of hope

51

also believe in Jesus, will be saved. She is wrong. She is revealing that she does not really believe the gospel. We must be saved through faith in Christ's sacrifice—God's way—or we cannot be saved at all. Do you pass the test? If you can be content to listen to someone who insists that anything must be added to faith, you do not understand the gospel.

THE SAVING WORK OF CHRIST IS FINISHED

There are no contingencies

Have you ever heard someone say, "I wish I were clairvoyant. I could look ahead at the stock market and make billions." No one has that ability. No one can speak with certainty about the outcome of current affairs and international crises before they happen.

That is why Christianity is so thrilling. Christ has died and is now risen as proof that God is permanently satisfied with the price paid for sin. There are no unknown factors. There is nothing up in the air. We need not sit with bated breath awaiting the outcome of God's decision concerning our salvation. There is nothing missing from God's perfect plan that would cause me to have to wait until the end of my life to discover it. Everything that we need in order to be saved is available to us now. There is not one thing left for us to do except see our need and claim, by faith alone, God's provision in His Son.

The conclusion of all of this is mind boggling. If there are no unknown factors, no circumstances about which anxious humanity must be uncertain, then we can know today that we are saved!

OUR RESPONSIBILITY—EXERCISE SAVING FAITH: SAVING FAITH IS CLAIMING BY PERSONAL CHOICE AND RELYING EXCLUSIVELY UPON CHRIST'S WORK ON THE CROSS TO BE SUFFICIENT PAYMENT FOR MY SIN

It's hard to put a "handle" on faith

The third great issue in evangelism involves our responsibility—faith. Here is the missing link—the missing ingredient—in many evangelistic presentations. We have so often been unable to communicate a rational understanding of what saving faith is. You will always know when you have failed in communicating the nature of faith. The person with whom you are talking will say, "I believe everything you have told me. I know I am a sinner. I believe that Jesus Christ is the Son of God who died to save me from the penalty of sin, but I'm still not sure I'm a Christian."

52

It is never easy to define faith. It is no small task to relate this precious idea to folks who have grown up in a religious atmosphere and have come to associate the trappings of churchianity with spirituality. Yet without faith it is impossible to please God (Hebrews 11:6). There are two aspects to our definition of saving faith. We must become intimately acquainted with both of them.

A CHOICE

First, saving faith involves a choice. No one will get to heaven against his will. We will not be able to say, "I'm here because my mother was a Christian, but I didn't really want to come." Every citizen of heaven will be a citizen by choice. God has given men the freedom of choice because He does not want His heaven to be populated by automatons and robots.

That, of course, is why we dare not use any gimmickry, high-pressure tactics, or Madison Avenue craftiness in our quest for souls. In order to exercise saving faith, a person must make a choice. When a person trusts Christ as Savior, his will is involved. There is a decision to be made. There is a promise to claim by choice.

One of the books of the Bible that emphasizes faith the most is the book of Hebrews. In it we read, "We . . . have a strong consolation, who have fled for refuge to lay hold upon the hope set before us" (Hebrews 6:18). That's the gospel truth. Christ has died for sin. God promises that all who come to Him through faith in Christ will be given the gift of eternal life. We are to lay hold of this promise for ourselves. We must take it, seize it, rest upon it. The choice is ours, but the choice must be made.

TRUST

Second, saving faith involves trust. That is why we define saving faith as claiming Christ by personal choice and *relying exclusively upon* Him. When we believe the gospel, we rely upon it alone as our hope of heaven. Faith is the ability to recline in the promise of God. That's right. Just as you recline in a sturdy chair that you know you can trust, you are to sit down in the assurance that Christ's blood was sufficient payment for all your sins.

Faith looks outside the individual, in space and time, to the historic event of Christ's crucifixion. It is that faith which becomes the channel that brings the benefits of Christ's substitutionary

Two basic aspects of saving faith

An act of the will is necessary

Faith necessitates exclusive reliance

work into my life. There are so many wonderful synonyms for *faith*: "trusting in," "relying upon," "grasping," "claiming," "seizing," "receiving," and "believing." All those words have one thing in common: they take something objective and outside ourselves and make it our own. We must take the promise of God and the finished work of Christ and make them our own. It is *history* when we say, "Christ died on Calvary." It is *theology* when we say, "Christ died on Calvary for sins." But it is *salvation* when we can exclaim, "Christ died on Calvary for *my* sins!"

Abraham's faith

The fourth chapter of Romans beautifully illustrates saving faith as trusting. The issue concerns Abraham, who was one hundred years old and who believed God's promise concerning the birth of Isaac. Medical science would not believe it, but God made a promise, and Abraham believed it. "He staggered not at the promise of God through unbelief, but was strong in faith, giving glory to God; and being fully persuaded that, what he [God] had promised, he was able also to perform" (Romans 4:20-21).

Learn this definition!

Saving faith, then, is claiming by personal choice and relying exclusively upon Christ's work on the cross to be sufficient payment for my sin. Again I ask you to learn well that definition of saving faith. Having taught this program of evangelism to hundreds of people, I find that the thing they appreciate more than any other is the definition of saving faith. I believe it can assist you tremendously. You will never be stumped again when someone asks you what it means to believe.

REVIEW OF CHAPTER 4
MASTERING THE THREE CRUCIAL ISSUES

1. Man's problem—All men are sinners, and sin separates us from God.
   a. The essence of sin:
      (1) Demanding our own way: "Me first!" (autonomy).
      (2) Defying the will of God: "Stay out of my life!" (rebellion).
      (3) Being driven by selfishness to do the wrong thing (unrighteousness).
   b. Death means separation:
      (1) Physical death: Separation of soul and body.
      (2) Spiritual death: Separation of my spirit from God's Spirit.
      (3) Second death: Separation forever from the presence of God in hell.
2. God's Solution—Calvary is God's only provision for man's sin.
   a. We are not saved by our performance, but by Christ's sacrifice. (Men have many false hopes that are rooted in performance—baptism, a moral life, church attendance, and so forth.)
   b. Calvary is God's only provision. The work of Christ cannot be mixed with religious rites or moral obligations.
   c. The saving work of Christ is finished. Because we do not await the outcome of any present contingencies, we can have peace with God today.
3. Our responsibility—exercise saving faith
   "Saving faith" is claiming by personal choice and relying exclusively upon Christ's work on the cross to be sufficient payment for my sin.
   a. Choice: A person's will is involved. The gift of eternal life is available to anyone who will claim it for himself.
   b. Trust: "Relying exclusively upon"—salvation is ours as we "recline in," or "sit down in," the promise of God.

When you know those three issues—in fact, when you know those three sentences—you know enough to lead a person to a saving knowledge of Christ.

Our task: to make these issues as clear as possible to whomever we are talking to and to persuade our listener that he can act immediately by claiming Christ as his Savior. This must not be done, however, until we are persuaded that the listener *understands* and believes these great issues.

ASSIGNMENTS

1. Review John 3:16, 1 Timothy 2:4, and 2 Peter 3:9 with your evangelism partner.
2. Learn Jeremiah 17:9, Romans 3:10, and Romans 3:23 word perfect.
3. Learn the three crucial issues in evangelism word perfect.

QUESTIONS FOR DISCUSSION

1. If the essence of the gospel is so basic that it can be communicated in three propositions, why do you think Christians are so confused about what the gospel is?

2. Write down a list of five implications that grow out of each of the three basic issues.

3. If Calvary is God's only provision for sin, why is it that many evangelists tell people to "accept Christ into your life" but never mention the only sure ground for peace with God?

4. It's time to ask you the most important question in life. Is your only hope of heaven rooted in the sufficiency of Christ's blood? Have you chosen to place your trust in Him? Ask yourself right now how you know where you will spend eternity.

PRAYER

Pray that God will give you clear insights about what really needs to be presented to a person in order for him to be saved. Pray that God will give you the grace to master these issues. Pray that you will never water down the priceless message of the gospel. Thank the Lord right now for sending His Son to die at Calvary to become your Savior.

5

Giving Your Personal Testimony

It could be that you have never given much thought to how you became a Christian. Perhaps you have grown up in a Christian home and have been saved since early childhood. Perhaps you cannot pinpoint when and where you first trusted Christ, even though you have perfect assurance that you are a Christian. These and many other factors might inhibit you from giving your personal testimony before others. I believe that more than half of our evangelical community does not know how to share a personal testimony. Most people don't even realize that they have one.

I remember a philosophy professor in college who began his lectures by saying, "Some people do not believe in the study of philosophy. They are being deceived; for philosophy simply involves the way we look at life and how we integrate those data of living into a consistent system. The question is not whether I have a philosophy. The question is rather whether the philosophy that I have is good or bad—consistent or inconsistent."

Many people sincerely believe that they have no personal testimony that is worthy of being told to an unsaved world. The truth is that *every* Christian has a testimony. Moreover, the testimony of *every* Christian is very important. It can play a vital role in leading men and women to Christ. The issue, then, is not whether I have a testimony, but how I can capsulize my testimony and organize it into an effective evangelistic tool. I trust that as you study this chapter, you not only will become excited about your personal testimony, but also will grasp the significance of your testimony when you are witnessing to others.

Every Christian has a testimony worth telling others about

We must develop a testimony into an evangelistic tool

THREE REASONS FOR
GIVING PERSONAL TESTIMONIES

A testimony is an individual's autobiographical account of how he personally came to know Christ as Savior and how his life has been transformed as a result of his conversion. There are three reasons for using your testimony in your witnessing.

First, when you use your testimony your audience cannot disagree with you. I have been in many homes and have shared the gospel many times. People feel perfectly free to disagree with anything I might say. They interrupt me and interact with me freely. But I have noticed a fascinating pattern over the past years. When I begin to give my personal testimony, the person to whom I am talking becomes strangely silent. He becomes engrossed in what I am saying. He has no desire to challenge my statements. He listens.

People cannot argue with personal experiences

As he hears me describe *my experiences*, he finds himself powerless—even desireless—to challenge me. In other words, I have not only a captive audience, but also the strategic advantage of being the only one who knows my experiences. You cannot argue about a person's experiences; you can argue only about ideas. Thus, I have a perfect device for sharing my faith in an uninterrupted fashion. My listener can accept my statements, because he cannot refute my experiences.

Second, in your testimony you can subtly say things that would be offensive if stated propositionally. Later in this chapter we will deal with six items that ought to be communicated every time you give your testimony. Any one of these items may be offensive to your listener. But you are just at the beginning of your presentation. At this stage you are not looking for a way to turn him off, but to turn him on.

A vehicle for telling the truth without offending

Let me give you an example of how a testimony can be used to communicate a truth that could be crushingly offensive if it were stated propositionally:

> Proposition: "Mr. Jones, I understand that you go to church every Sunday. I must inform you that going to church won't save you or anybody else."
>
> Testimony: "All my life I had attended church faithfully. Yet my soul ached for a deeper reality. Then I heard the gospel. Suddenly I discovered that churches cannot save; only the Lord Jesus can!"

58

Which of the above is likely to be most offensive? Yet, are not both statements communicating the truth that religion doesn't save? Again, the issue is how to communicate truth in an uncompromising way that will leave the listener asking for more.

Third, a testimony is designed to whet one's appetite for more. We urge people to confine their testimonies to three minutes. There is a reason for that. The testimony is not designed to lead men to Christ; its purpose is to create an interest and incite a curiosity that make them want to know more about the faith.

In our sequence of presentation, the sharing of one's testimony forms an important bridge. It links a discussion of the listener's personal and secular views to your presentation of gospel facts. It is a bridge to cross if one is going to gain a hearing for the gospel. It is not to become a substitute for the gospel presentation itself. You will have succeeded in your purpose if, after you have given your testimony, the listener responds by saying: "Wow! That is absolutely fascinating! Won't you tell me more?"

THE OUTLINE OF YOUR TESTIMONY

After considerable experimentation, I'm convinced that a simple chronological approach to your salvation experience is the most efficient form of testimony. Your task is to unfold the highlights of three distinct periods of your life:

1. What your life was like before you became a Christian.

2. What happened the day you trusted Christ.

3. How Christ has changed your life since that day.

WHAT YOUR LIFE WAS LIKE
BEFORE YOU BECAME A CHRISTIAN

If you were saved at an early age, it will not do for you to recite what a terrible sinner you were. Be honest with people. Tell them that you had no hang-ups, but that even at an early age you knew that something was wrong. You had a need. You were afraid of God, afraid to die. If you have become a Christian as an adult, your story will be much different. You can stress the restlessness of your unsaved past. If you are an intellectual, you can talk about the emptiness of your studies. If you are a socialite, you can tell your listeners that you have known hundreds of people, but you still felt alone. If you were intemperate, you can relate

Goal: "I want to hear more!"

A testimony in three parts

Before: Frustration

59

that you had tried everything—sex, alcohol, and drugs—but found no fulfillment. If you were a religionist, you can communicate the enslavement of religion apart from the grace of God. Be creative, but in your own way you must communicate that the unsaved life left you unfulfilled and wanting.

WHAT HAPPENED THE DAY YOU TRUSTED CHRIST

Crisis: What really happened?

Everyone is puzzled by the mystery of conversion. To this day I listened with great rapture to anyone who shares his testimony. All the new members of our church give their testimonies before our entire congregation. It is my favorite service. I am never bored. There are so many ways that people have come to Christ.

Yet, in every case, something triggered the decision. It may have been a tragedy, or a special service, or a conversation with a friend. It may have been bizarre or very natural. You must tell with precision what happened on that great day that your life was changed. There came a moment when you saw the issue. What was that issue? What was your response? What made the difference? How did you pass from death to life?

HOW CHRIST HAS CHANGED YOUR LIFE SINCE THAT DAY

After: Christ has changed my life

This, of course, is the most satisfying part of a testimony. It is thrilling to look a person in the eye and tell him that you are not the man you used to be. Christ changes our lives! "If any man be in Christ, he is a new creature: old things are passed away; behold, all things are become new" (2 Corinthians 5:17).

People will look at you in utter amazement as you tell about your peace, your joy, your new desires, and your purpose for living. You will have great satisfaction in the knowledge that no man apart from Christ shares your inner contentment. Some will look respectable—indeed, some will live a life that is outwardly enviable—but all will be hurting on the inside.

No one can argue with a changed life. It is the most convincing demonstration of the truth of Christianity. But don't brag about yourself. Give glory to God. Concentrate on what He is doing. People can easily detect the difference between cocky bragging and genuine joy and thanksgiving. Do not stress your accomplishments. Major on changed attitudes and perspectives. But by all means, glory in your assurance. This will absolutely amaze the average religious listener. He has no sure hope. He has no certainty in his religion.

60

BASIC ISSUES IN EVERY TESTIMONY

Although the historical data of each testimony will vary greatly, all testimonies ought to include the three basic issues of the gospel. These basic issues can be reported to your listeners as personal discoveries. In other words, you have not merely done research into the doctrines of Christianity, you have uncovered some important insights into life through your own personal experiences. Your testimony ought to include:

1. The fact that you discovered that you were a sinner.

2. The fact that you discovered that Jesus Christ died for your sin.

3. The fact that now you know the delightful certainty of faith.

A SAMPLE TESTIMONY

The following is the story of my own conversion. Please read it carefully and try to discover the main points I am trying to communicate.

From my earliest childhood, I discovered that I had a very religious bent. My parents would take me to Sunday school regularly. When I became a teenager, I joined the adult choir. I was proud of myself!

For a while, everything seemed all right. Then I began to wonder what our church really stood for. It was a pretty little church. Its people were very friendly. But I became troubled by my inability to discover its central message.

Every year they talked about Christ's coming to earth at Christmas. Every Easter they would talk about Christ on the cross. But why did He come? Why did Christ die? These were questions for which I had no answer. I became president of the church youth group, and I even preached a sermon, but by that time I could see that I was only going through the motions, playing a game. I felt alone, unsure, and unfulfilled. My church was failing to meet my need.

After I entered high school, I became engrossed in playing football. In my school the football players had it made. Football was becoming a way of life. Then things began to happen. A cute little blonde invited me to a high school Bible club. What nerve she had! Didn't she understand that football and religion don't mix? She was very gracious but very persistent. I said no to her for six months. Finally, I ran out of noes and agreed to go. I shall never forget that experience.

At the club meeting I met sixty of the most attractive kids I had ever seen. Their eyes

As you read my testimony, underline the basic truths that I am trying to communicate

seemed to glow with brightness. Their smiles were warm and transparent. The meeting began. One by one, kids would get up and say something. One stood to his feet and said, "I'm so glad I trusted Christ as my Savior. Things are different now!" I had never heard anything like that in sixteen years of going to church. Another said, "Kids, we've got to pray for Bob's parents. They don't understand his new faith." Another said, "Oh, the Lord is so wonderful! I just had to stand up and thank Him for sending His Son, Jesus Christ, to die for me!"

After forty-five minutes of that kind of sharing, I was absolutely shaken. I was suddenly aware of a whole new world. From that first encounter, I began slowly to put the pieces together. Finally, one day six months later, I read a book about God's amazing grace. My heart began to melt as my mind began to understand the Christian faith. Remember when I said that I had always been puzzled about why Christ came to earth and why He died on the cross? Now I understood! He died for me! He knew I was a sinner—powerless to save myself. He took my place on Calvary's cross. That night I knelt down by my bed and told the Lord that I was a sinner who needed a Savior. I told Him that I believed He sent His Son to die for me. I claimed Christ's blood as payment for my sin—and for the first time in sixteen years I had peace with God.

From that moment on, my life began to change. I still had plenty of problems, but I could face each of those problems from a new perspective! I began to love my Bible; I began to crave the fellowship of other Christians. Ultimately, the Lord led me into full-time service for Him. God is so good. I am so happy. Now life is so full. I trusted Christ as my Savior more than sixteen years ago. Perhaps the most remarkable thing of all is that I have never doubted once in all those years that I belong to the Lord. I know I'm going to heaven. Oh, by the way, you remember that cute little girl who invited me out to Bible club? She's now my wife and the mother of our three children. Yes, I believe God has a wonderful plan for every life.

SIX FACTS MY TESTIMONY WAS DESIGNED TO COMMUNICATE

There are six facts my testimony was designed to communicate. *First, religion doesn't save.* Religion has become the crutch of many people. If you ask them whether they are Christians, they respond, "Yes, I go to church." No one is ready for the gospel until he despairs of religion. We live in a day when an entire genera-

Religion doesn't save

tion is being turned off by the organized church. As witnesses of Christ, we must take advantage of this opportunity before disillusioned people have become hardened in sin and perversity.

Our duty is to spread the message that only Christ can save. Churches never can. Think clearly about your life. Perhaps you were like me. I had attended a nice church. But it offered me no gospel. What was your impression of Christianity in your old church? Remember, religious people can almost fool themselves into being satisfied that as long as they are faithful to their church it will be well with their souls. They are capable of deceiving themselves. But in their hearts they long for greater assurance. So long as people depend on religious exercises instead of the sufficiency of Christ, they will never know full assurance.

Second, most people have no purpose for living. Stress in your testimony that life apart from a saving knowledge of Christ has no ultimately satisfying purpose. Even the most successful businessmen will say, "Why am I here? What am I killing myself for?" In America today most people are purposeless. Even those who do a great deal of partying wake up only to find that they have no reason to be alive. If you were like that before you became a Christian, say so, because millions of people feel just the way you did.

Life without Christ has no purpose

Third, at a point in time, I passed from death to life. Much of our present religious world believes that we slowly evolve into righteous human beings. Everything is gradual. Everything is blurry. Men and women become followers of God by osmosis. That is a fallacy. We were born in sin. If we want to be "in Christ," there must come a moment when we cross the bridge, or make a decision. "Verily, verily, I say unto you, He that heareth my word, and believeth on him that sent me, hath everlasting life, and shall not come into condemnation, but is passed from death unto life" (John 5:24).

A Christian has passed from death to life

Fourth, I placed my trust in the work of Christ on the cross. You will be spending a great deal of time trying to explain substitution in any great length. You dare not leave it out any time you give your testimony. In the end, it is the sufficiency of Christ's work alone—not the way I claim it—that brings peace to my soul. Stress that you had to claim God's perfect provision for yourself.

A Christian trusts the work of Christ

Fifth, things are different now. Give God the glory. You are still a sinner saved by grace. You

Christ makes a difference

still have feet of clay. You still battle the flesh. Admit that you have problems, but don't emphasize them or give the impression that you are proud of them. You have changed. The Christian life has problems, but it also has victories. If your life has no victory in it, I seriously doubt that you will ever be able to lead someone to Christ. There must be a consciousness of God at work in your life. Share this with joy.

Sixth, I am sure I am going to heaven. You dare never omit this certainty from your testimony. It absolutely slays the unregenerate man. He will say, "No one knows for sure! It is impossible! How presumptuous you are!" But in his heart of hearts he will long for your confidence. Your peace will overwhelm him. This is what separates believers from unbelievers: Christians know they are going to heaven. Others can only hope.

Communicate assurance!

ISSUES TO AVOID WHEN GIVING YOUR TESTIMONY

Keep before you the fundamental purpose of your testimony. It is to intrigue and fascinate your listener. It ought to make him want to hear more. With that in mind, common sense will tell you what to avoid. Here are a few suggestions.

Don't get too complicated. Keep your theological vocabulary to a minimum. Come to a period often. (Some people can make a testimony into one long, continuous sentence.) Be sure your sequence of thought follows a logical progression. Pace yourself, and keep the pace brisk. It is better to emphasize a few things clearly than to try to include too much in your testimony.

Goal: You want your listener to ask for more

Stick to the point. One person began like this: "It all started with my cousin Mike. Actually, he isn't my cousin, he's my wife's second cousin. Of course, that was my previous wife who died in 1942 from lead poisoning." Need I say more? I think you get the point perfectly.

Don't ask questions. We have already stated that the virtue of sharing your testimony is that you will have a captive audience who will sit quietly and never think to interrupt you. Once you ask your listener a question, the spell is broken and you may have a very difficult time getting him back on the track.

Avoid denominational name-calling. Some people believe it is necessary to mention that they are from a Roman Catholic or Lutheran background. I do not fault them for this. But don't mention names needlessly. Also, don't drag the main-line denominations through the mud and call the pastors of these churches heretics. Some people who have a genuine desire to hear the truth will never give you a chance to tell it if you belittle denominations.

Your first sentence is crucial. Most of us give our testimonies in church rather than among unbelievers. That is unfortunate. We get trapped into habits. For example, we begin our story like this: "Before I got saved . . ." Don't ever begin your testimony that way when you are with an unbeliever. Avoid clichés. Be provocative. One young lady who took our training used her creativity to begin her testimony like this: "Ever since I can remember, I have always wanted to be an artist." Won't that draw your attention?

Don't glory in former depravity. Don't be afraid to be honest about your past life. But glory in Christ and in your new life. You will win your audience not by the grotesqueness of your details but by the genuiness of your love for Christ.

REVIEW OF CHAPTER 5
GIVING YOUR PERSONAL TESTIMONY

KEYS TO WRITING YOUR TESTIMONY

1. The outline of your testimony
   a. What you were like before you became a Christian
   b. What happened the day you received Christ (What made the difference?)
   c. How Christ changed your life
2. Basic issues in every testimony
   a. You discovered that you were a sinner
   b. Christ died for your sin
   c. You are certain of your belief—you know that you are saved—you have no doubt
3. What your testimony should subtly communicate
   a. Religion doesn't save
   b. Most people have no purpose—use yourself as the example
   c. At a point in *time* you passed from death to life
   d. Christ died—you put faith in that
   e. Things are different now
   f. You are sure that you are going to heaven

NOTE: Remember, when you share your own personal experience, that you have a captive audience who will not argue (for they cannot refute your experience). You can say things here that would be offensive if stated propositionally. The point of your testimony is not to communicate everything you know about the Bible, but to create an interest and incite a curiosity that make men want to know more about the faith.

ASSIGNMENTS

1. Review your memory verses with your evangelism partner.
2. Your memory assignment for this week: Ezekiel 18:4 and Romans 6:23.
3. Write out your personal testimony. Do it carefully and prayerfully. Try to complete it on one side of a sheet of paper. Try to condense it into a three-minute presentation. Say it aloud (without looking at the paper) to your partner.

QUESTIONS FOR DISCUSSION

1. As you listen to the testimony of your partner, evaluate it:
   a. Was I drawn by what he said?
   b. Was his delivery winsome?
   c. Did he offend me?
   d. Did I understand what he said?
   e. If he were a stranger to me, would I want him to tell me more?
2. Evaluate your own thoughts as you give your testimony. Are you saying what you really want to communicate?

PRAYER

Thank the Lord Jesus that He has given you a testimony. Your life is changed! Ask Him for many opportunities to present your testimony to unsaved men and women.

6

A Comprehensive Approach to Presenting the Gospel

Phase One: From the First Minute of Conversation to the Discernment of a Person's Need

The next three chapters present a continuous sequence. They begin as you approach the home of a stranger. They conclude with a person's gaining assurance of his salvation. They assume that you know little about your prospect. It is important to realize that you must begin your witness at a point of common interest. If you are presenting the gospel of Christ to a relative or close friend, much of the material in this chapter can be bypassed. You may, in that case, want to begin by telling him your testimony. You may even want to begin by asking him the two basic questions that open the door to the presentation of the gospel. Start where you must. Never feel compelled to begin with, "Hello, my name is. . . ." Common sense will be your best guide.

I know I speak for thousands of pastors as I express my indebtedness to Dr. James Kennedy, pastor of the Coral Ridge Presbyterian Church in Fort Lauderdale, Florida, for convincing me that it is worthwhile to map out a comprehensive strategy that begins with your approaching a prospect's home and concludes with your leaving that home. In the strategy that I am about to present, I have adopted from Dr. Kennedy the invitation and the four questions that set the stage for presenting the gospel.

The key to our strategy is *bridge building*. By that I mean the ability to make a change in the conversation which is imperceptible to your listener. At every key point in your presentation, a

Dr. Kennedy's helpful questions

bridge can be built that makes your entire communication natural. If your bridges are well built, the listener will never dream that you are following a clearly defined outline. Everything you say will sound spontaneous.

We begin, now, to detail our approach. At the end of chapter eight, we will present an overall summary, which we trust you will study thoroughly.

THE INTRODUCTION

At our church we make evangelistic calls every Tuesday night of the year. We meet at 7:15 sharp. The assignment cards are distributed. We sing a chorus, have a word of prayer, and are on our way by 7:30 sharp.

On the way to the prospect's house, our team of evangelists get to know each other better. We have tried all kinds of team combinations. Our conclusion is that ladies should go with ladies, men with men. Occasionally, one trainer will take a couple with him. This is a wonderful opportunity for Christian fellowship. The fringe benefit of our program is that every time people go witnessing they make a friend. There is a wonderful sense of common concern and genuine spiritual fellowship among our people.

As the team approaches the home, someone leads in prayer. We encourage the team members to do this before they arrive in front of the house. ("Lord, tonight you have brought us to this particular place for a reason. You are going to work in us and through us tonight. Thank you for the excitement of being able to depend on You. We give You our fears and claim Your power.") The walk to the front door ought to be a very optimistic time. If you are optimists, it will show on your faces when someone comes to the door.

A time for optimism

Our people are trained to believe that the first minute of conversation is absolutely the most crucial. If we fail here, we may never get a second chance. You must know exactly what you are going to say when someone comes to the door. Your first sentences ought to sound something like this:

The first minute is critical

> "Mr. Brown? Hello, my name is Dick Sisson, and this is Tom Gibson. We are from the North Side Gospel Center. We are happy to have your son, Bobby, in our Pals club. I would love to be able to take a few minutes to explain to you why we have a club for boys. May we come in for a moment?"

68

In that brief introduction, I have accomplished five objectives.

1. I have made the person I am talking to aware that I know his name. That establishes my visit as something other than a random neighborhood canvass. I am there expressly to see him.

2. I have stated my name unashamedly. I want more than an impersonal meeting at the door. I want to establish a friendship.

3. I have relieved the person's mind about whom I represent. I am a part of a friendly neighborhood church. That is important, because the cultists are in the doorbell-ringing business, also. Now the person I am talking to knows that I am not a cultist.

4. I have shown the person I am talking to that there is a reason for my visit. That is an incalculable advantage. It has opened a door that otherwise might be shut. I know about his son, Bobby. Bobby comes to our Pals club. I want to share with Bobby's parents the reason we have a boys club.

It is a wonderful asset to have a reason for your visit. Most of our calls are made to the parents of the five hundred young people who attend our Awana clubs each week. We also visit the homes of our Sunday school visitors, the children we pick up on bus routes, and the visitors who attend our services. When we run low on prospects, we ask each of our trainers to come up with his own prospects and his reasons for visiting.

5. I have taken the initiative of inviting us in. Most people who are not expecting company feel embarrassed about letting them into their homes. If you don't take the initiative, you will probably spend your time on the front porch.

Always have a purpose for visiting

PRELIMINARY DISCUSSION

After you have introduced yourself and broken the ice, you should talk casually for a while. You need to establish rapport with your host. Don't proceed with the gospel until you feel comfortable with him and he feels comfortable with you. It may take just a few minutes, but sometimes it may take longer.

From the moment you enter, force your mind to be active. Look for hints of personal interest, such as trophies, handmade craft projects, paintings, rugs, or hobbies. You are looking for conversational topics that come close to the core of a person's life. What you are really saying is: "I want to get to know you. Tell me something about yourself." Certain subjects naturally lend them-

Don't witness until you have developed a basic rapport

selves to rapport building. Things that people like to talk about are interesting furnishings, family relationships, current events, their personal backgrounds, and their personal interests.

We live in a world where almost no one cares what other people think. As you demonstrate that you care, you will be amazed at how quickly a total stranger opens up to you. And care you must. Be a good listener. Encourage the prospect to talk. Everyone enjoys talking about himself and his interests. Now that everyone is relaxing, it is time to build your first bridge.

THE PERSON'S RELIGIOUS LIFE

"Mr. Brown, did you ever attend a church club like Bobby's? In what church did you grow up?"

Those questions are vital, not only because they introduce the whole arena of spiritual things, but also because the answers give you immediate insight into the other person's spiritual condition. Much comes to the surface about what a person really believes when he begins to talk about the churches he has attended. Store his remarks in your memory bank. They may become invaluable later.

Do not try to encourage criticism. It would be easy for you to begin to bait a person. It will not help your purposes whatsoever to have him go into elaborate details about the phonies and hypocrites of the religious establishment. You must become genuinely interested in his appraisal of his own church background. Sympathize with shortcomings. Smile at blessings. Now it is time to build another bridge.

YOUR CHURCH'S MINISTRY

"Mr. Brown, I am always fascinated when I hear someone talk about his church. Perhaps that's because I love ours so much. I am very glad that we have an exciting boys' club that Bobby can attend."

This last sentence could just as easily have been, "I am very glad that we have an exciting Sunday school that Susie can visit occasionally," or, "I'm very glad that you visited our morning service last week." You have just linked that home to your church. Now you have the opportunity to discuss the prospect's attitude toward your church and your reasons for being a church. This discussion will flow from three questions.

1. "How did Bobby start coming to Pals?" This is the most basic and least offensive question

that you can ask to solicit a response concerning your church.

2. "I'd love to know how Bobby feels about Pals." For the first time you are asking for an evaluation of part of your church's program. Be prepared for anything. But almost all children love to be a part of a weekday club program or an exciting Sunday school. Moreover, almost every parent is thankful that his children enjoy being involved in a church.

3. "Do you know why we have a Pals club?" (Or "a Sunday school," or "a bus ministry.") Here is the next critical bridge. You have been talking about the surface realities of your youth program or about your worship services. Now you begin to go below the surface. You are about to lead that person into the great spiritual issues of life.

"Actually, the reason we have a Pals club is the very same reason that we have a church. We want to do the will of the Lord Jesus Christ. His plan for His church is wonderful. He asks us to show men and women how to be sure of eternal life and how to enjoy a satisfying and abundant life in this world.

This question of purpose is a key bridge into giving your testimony

YOUR PERSONAL TESTIMONY

Now you can launch your testimony by admitting that your own life has not always been satisfying. Remember, the outline of your testimony is simple: what your life was like before you trusted Christ as your Savior, what made the difference at the point of decision, and how Christ has changed your life since then. As you talk, look for signs of genuine interest and conviction in the other person.

(If you were saved at a young age, say: "I've certainly found this to be true.")

Speak with quiet confidence. Let the inner joy that flows from a redeemed heart become apparent. That is the key to an effective presentation of your testimony. It is a valuable opportunity to create an appetite in an unsaved person for a message that sets people free and makes them happy. It is always my prayer that my testimony will have the same effect on the listener as cold water poured over the parched tongue of a man dying of thirst. Be sure to include the basics:

1. Religion does not save anyone.
2. Life once was empty, unsatisfying, purposeless.
3. I heard a message that changed my life—the message of Calvary.
4. I passed from death to life.

5. Now I'm sure that I'm going to heaven.
6. Christ has made a wonderful difference in my life.

Make truth come alive!

Your testimony can make theology come to life. It is not stuff from a book. It is reality! I'm amazed at how personal testimony was used in the Bible. Andrew met the Savior. His first thought was to tell his brother, Peter. He ran to him and shouted, "Peter, we have found the Messiah!" and he brought him to Jesus. A Samaritan woman placed her faith in Christ, then ran to tell her whole village about it. "Come, see a man who told me all the things I ever did!" A man blind from birth was healed. Jesus' critics told the man to deny that Christ did it by the power of God. His response was, "Whether He is a sinner I know not, but one thing I know—that I was blind, and now I see!" Paul effectively shared his personal testimony with King Agrippa, and the king responded, "Almost thou persuadest me to be a Christian" (Acts 26:28).

That is exactly the purpose of a testimony. It almost persuades; it fascinates and convicts; but it must be followed by something more substantial and systematic. It is time to present the gospel. The most exciting hour of your week is underway. Your adrenaline is flowing. But how do you go from your testimony to the systematic presentation of the gospel? How do you know that a person even needs the gospel? It is time for you to master the two most significant questions you will ever learn. They constitute the most essential bridge in your entire presentation.

TWO POWERFUL QUESTIONS

You have been giving your testimony. You want the listener to know that you are saved. But now you want to discover if he is saved. Your opportunity to ask these questions can come about quite naturally. "I've been talking about myself," you say. "I'd really like to know more about you. Do you mind if I ask you a question?"

In four years of following this pattern, I've never been told by anyone that he minded. I ask, "Have you come to the place in your spiritual life that you could say for sure that if you were to die today you know you would go to heaven?"

The great question (Can be answered by yes or no)

We call that the *general question*. It is general because it can be answered by a simple yes or no. It forces the listener to examine his own life. He can no longer evade the issue. Usually, however, you will not receive a simple yes or no. The answer more likely will be, "Well, I don't think any-one can know that for sure," or "I would like to think so," or "Sometimes I feel as if I would and sometimes I feel as if I wouldn't." No matter what response you receive, you then ask the second question.

"That's very interesting. Perhaps I could help you to clarify your thoughts with another ques-tion. Suppose you were to die today and stand before God, and He should ask you, 'Mr. Brown, why should I let you into my heaven?' What would your answer be?"

That is the *specific question*. It cannot be an-swered with a simple yes or no. A person must commit himself. He must search out his true hope of heaven. In the hundreds of times that I have asked that question, I have never had an unsaved listener "fake it" and give me the right answer. The right answer, of course, is, "I would tell Him that although I am a sinner and cannot do any-thing to save myself, I have placed my trust in His Son's work on Calvary's cross, and I rest my hope on the certainty of His promise."

But that is usually not the answer I receive. Here are nine typical responses:

1. "I have always tried to do my best."
2. "I think I am as worthy as the next guy."
3. "I've tried to do right by my family."
4. "I haven't missed church in fifty years!"
5. "I believe in God."
6. "No loving God would deny people a place in heaven."
7. "I try to live up to the Ten Commandments."
8. "I've been baptized and confirmed."
9. "My parents always brought me up to fear and honor the Lord."

The answer is given. Now you must solidify that answer in the person's mind. He has never thought of the question before. He is speaking off the top of his head. It is important to make him very conscious of his answer. Often, when one of our people presents the message of grace and begins to discuss the matter of making a decision, the listener will say, "Well, I've always believed in what you are saying."

In a sense, he has. There are very few Ameri-cans who have not heard Christian answers at various times in their lives. Radio and television programs have reached millions. Churches, even if they are not evangelical, teach concepts that cover the subjects of Christ, sin, heaven, Calvary, and faith. Many people are convinced that they

The specific question (Demands a substantive response)

Be sure to ask the person to repeat his answer

have always believed in the Lord Jesus Christ. This is especially true of people from main-line denominations.

They are using *believe* in a different way. That Christ lived and died and performed miracles is acknowledged generally. But the Bible uses belief in a very specific sense. *We believe when we rest our hope in something.* Our faith is not vague mental assent. It is conscious, willful trust.

Many who give hopelessly inadequate answers to the specific question will later say that they believe. Here is the most painful part of sharing the gospel. We must tenderly expose the inconsistency of their saying that they believe what we share although they had previously given a deficient answer to the question about their hope of heaven.

If, in response to the specific question, the person gives a deficient answer and later says that he believes, even if you suspect that he doesn't, you will have no choice but to accept his statement of belief or call him a liar, unless you have previously clarified and made him understand his answer. Therefore, always ask him to repeat his answer.

"Now let me see if I understand you accurately, Mr. Brown," you say. "If you were to stand before God and He should ask you, 'Why should I let you into my heaven,' you would say, 'Because I always tried to live a godly life and do the best I can.' Is that your answer?"

"Yes it is," he will say.

At this point, a zealous witness could make a tragic mistake. He could start a holy war. He could respond, "Well, I just want you to know that you are all wrong!" But that is not the way to turn a wrong answer into a wonderful opportunity. Say, "Mr. Brown, I knew nothing about you when I came here tonight, but now I know that I have good news for you."

Turn a minus into a plus

You have just succeeded in turning a minus into a plus. His insufficient response becomes your cue for sharing the precious gospel of the grace of God. You have built another bridge.

REVIEW OF CHAPTER 6
A COMPREHENSIVE APPROACH TO
PRESENTING THE GOSPEL

PHASE ONE: FROM THE FIRST MINUTE OF CONVERSATION TO THE DISCERNMENT OF A PERSON'S NEED

1. Introduction

   "Hello, my name is Dick Sisson and I'm from the North Side Gospel Center. We are happy to have your son, Bobby, in our Pals club. I would love to be able to take a few minutes to explain to you why we have a club for boys. May I come in for a moment?"

   a. State your name immediately.
   b. Also, identify your church unapologetically. (This will put at ease people who fear that you might be a cultist who travels the neighborhood circuit.)
   c. Share your *purpose*.

2. The person's secular life

   a. There is one huge purpose for discussing the person's secular life: the establishment of comfort and rapport with each other. Do not go deeper into your presentation until you feel that both of you are comfortable.
   b. Key: Look for hints of personal interest (trophies, handmade items, hobbies). Ask questions as close to the core of the person's life as you can. You are really saying: "Tell me something about you."
      (1) Interesting furnishings
      (2) Family relationships
      (3) Current events
      (4) The person's personal background
      (5) The person's personal interests

3. The person's religious life

   "What church did you attend back in Virginia?" (This is a very important question. You will probably get some clues to the person's spiritual condition right here.)

   a. Do not try to encourage criticism.
   b. Be genuinely interested in the person's appraisal of his church background.

4. Your church

   The discussion of your church is one of the crucial *bridges* in the gospel presentation. Know well the three questions that follow.

   a. "How did Bobby start coming to Pals?" ("How did you happen to visit our church several weeks ago?" "How did Sue hear about our Sunday school?") The key here is to take advantage of the person's association with your church.
   b. "How does he like Pals?" ("How did you enjoy our morning worship service?")

c. The reason for your church. ("Do you know why we have a Pals club in our church? Christ put His church into the world to point men and women to eternal life. And yet few people are satisfied with their lives.")

5. Your personal testimony

"That was certainly true of my life. . ."

Remember, your testimony is your opportunity to create an appetite for more, to demonstrate an assurance of personal salvation, and to relate a personal experience with which one cannot argue. Be sure to communicate these facts:

    a. Religion doesn't save anyone.
    b. Life used to be empty, unsatisfying, purposeless.
    c. I heard a message that changed my life—the message of Calvary.
    d. At a point in time, I passed from death to life.
    e. Now I'm *sure* that I'm going to heaven.
    f. Christ has made a wonderful difference in my life.

6. Two powerful questions

"Say, I've been talking about myself! May I ask you a question?"

    a. *General Question* (it can be answered by a simple yes or no): "Have you come to the place in your own spiritual life where you know for certain that if you were to die today you would go to heaven?"
    b. *Specific Question* (it cannot be answered by a yes or no): "Suppose you were to die tonight and stand before God, and He were to say to you: 'Why should I let you into My heaven?' What would your answer be?"
       (1) Have him clarify or *repeat* his answer.
       (2) "Mrs. Jones, now I know that I have some good news for you."

ASSIGNMENTS

1. By the end of the next chapter, you will understand the basic gospel presentation. You must be able to support the gospel outline with memorized Scripture verses. Therefore, take time to go over all the verses you have learned thus far with your evangelism partner.
2. Memorize:

Romans 5:8	1 Peter 2:24
2 Corinthians 5:21	1 Peter 3:18
1 Peter 1:18-19	

QUESTIONS FOR DISCUSSION

1. Stand in front of a full-length mirror. Ask yourself this question, "If I came to the front door of my house, would I let me in?"
2. What causes people to be afraid of strangers at the door? What can we do to alleviate their fears?
3. Does a person's appearance affect his chances of gaining a hearing?
4. What do you see in your own house that could be used as a point of conversational interest?
5. Ask your evangelism partner if the bridge-building devices in this chapter are really workable.

PRAYER

Pray that the preciousness of Christ will be so real to you that your joy and winsomeness will be instantly obvious to the strangers you meet.

7

A Comprehensive Approach to Presenting the Gospel

Phase Two: Presenting the Five Basic Truths of the Gospel

For two thousand years, the saints of God have gladly forfeited their lives for the gospel of grace. It is worthy of their sacrifices. It is the most important communication ever to reach the ears of mankind.

The gospel of grace is enigmatic. It is precise, yet it can easily be perverted. Men pervert the good news in several ways. I would not be a good steward of the gospel if I did not clearly identify these perversions: Men are continually trying to add human effort to the gospel. Some teach that we must base our salvation on personal experiences rather than upon the objective, unchangeable promise of God. Others insist that salvation is not eternally sure, so we must strive to keep it. But by far, the most common perversion is the teaching that we must give up something in order to receive eternal life.

In a previous chapter, we became acquainted with the three great issues in evangelism. I trust you can now quote them word perfect. Let's review them together.

1. Man's Problem: All men are sinners, and sin separates us from God.
2. God's solution: Calvary is God's only provision for man's sin.
3. Our Responsibility: Exercise saving faith. Saving faith is claiming by personal choice and relying exclusively upon Christ's work on the cross to be sufficient payment for our sin.

Think for a moment. Ask yourself, What do I really want to communicate about Christ? What

Though the gospel is precise, it can easily be perverted and still sound Christian

Saturate yourself with these basics

77

makes the gospel such good news? How does it change men's lives? Why do we call it the gospel of the grace of God?

I'll never forget a story that I heard recently. A young man was listening to a man in his eighties. The old man could hardly talk. It was difficult to understand his speech. Yet he had an irresistible glow in his eyes. The old man said, "I am old now, but I have lived half my life for the Lord Jesus Christ. I was saved when I was over forty years old. In the course of the last forty years of my life, the Lord has taught me three things."

The young man was very interested. It would be wonderful if he could learn in four minutes what this old man had learned in forty years. He listened intently.

Three profitable lessons

"Yes, these are the three lessons that the Lord has taught me: First, men and women cannot lift a finger to save themselves. Second, God never intended for them to try. Third, Christ has done it all."

At that moment, the young man understood grace. Grace means that there are no performance conditions to salvation. There are no strings attached. Paul said it perfectly, "Being justified freely by his grace through the redemption that is in Christ Jesus: whom God hath set forth to be a propitiation [that is, a divine satisfaction, a basis upon which sins can now be forgiven] through faith in his blood" (Romans 3:24-25a).

No performance conditions in order to be saved

Do you see the distinctives of the message of grace? God saves men just as they are. The Holy Spirit convicts them of the bad news. Men are lost, hell-deserving sinners. They have no power to deal with their own sins. God sends a witness to tell them the good news—to open men's eyes in hope—as they see that Jesus Christ has already paid for the sins of the world. God does not save men as they surrender their lives to Him. Men surrender their lives to Him because they are saved. The only condition for salvation is the awareness of lostness—of sin and its awful consequences—and the willingness to place our faith in the sufficiency of Calvary's sacrifice.

Read this paragraph several times

For hundreds of years, this message has been ridiculed by its adversaries as "easy believism" because it does not require men to change their lives in order to get saved. The opponents of grace will never understand that the only cause of a truly changed life is a happy, joyful, liberated, redeemed heart.

What is "easy believism"?

I have been criticized for not calling men to repentance. But that is not true. I do call men to repentance. It is the meaning of the word *repentance* that causes misunderstandings. Some say repentance means the willingness to turn from all your sins and make Jesus Christ the Lord of every area of your life. That is not true. Repentance means a change of mind. God asks me to change my mind about my sin, His Son, and Christ's blood. Once I thought I was OK. I thought that I could get to heaven by being good. I didn't have to depend on the work of Christ. Then I repented. I discovered that I couldn't save myself. I was lost. I needed a Savior. I looked in faith to Jesus.

Perhaps there is no better definition of repentance in the Bible than that which is found in the story of the prodigal son. The boy said to his father, "Give me all that is mine!" He went to a foreign country and wasted his fortune on riotous living. Soon he was penniless. He got a job feeding pigs. He saw them eating better than he did.

The lad began to take stock of his life. He reached the moment of repentance, in the words of Luke, "when he came to himself" (Luke 15:17)! Here is repentance. The young man began to see things as they really were.

It was necessary for us to digress for these few pages so that you see clearly the things that must be presented as you tell people about Christ. Now we will return to where we ended the last chapter.

You must understand that the following material merely demonstrates the way I am most comfortable in putting flesh on the skeleton of the gospel. Your task is to understand and memorize the five-point outline of the gospel. Then memorize support verses that prove your points. Master your bridge-building sentences and your key concept for each point. After that, it is all yours. Let your personality determine your illustrations. I hope that the following pages will give you insight into how to allow your personality to fit within the presentation of a fixed body of truth.

"Mr. Brown, I didn't know much about you when I came here tonight, but now I know that I have good news for you." This is where we left off in the last chapter. Now ask, "Do you mind if I take a few minutes to tell you what I have discovered in my Bible about the answers to the questions I have just asked? I believe that almost everything the Bible teaches about going to heaven can be crystallized into five important truths. May I tell them to you?"

Repentance: coming to one's senses—seeing things as they really are

Your task in mastering this material

Use the following outline, verses, and selected illustrations as you proceed.

Here is the information to be mastered if your presentation is going to flow naturally

1. GOD IS GOOD, A GOD OF LOVE, WHO DOES NOT WANT ANYONE TO PERISH

Support verses: John 3:16; 1 Timothy 2:4; 2 Peter 3:9

Key concept: The goodness of God. He wants to save everyone.

Illustrations: a. Woman running from a fortune
b. God pictured by some as a concentration camp officer
c. Obstacles in our path—an act of love

Bridge: "Look around you. God doesn't want anyone to perish, yet there are signs of death everywhere. Men are perishing. Why?"

SUPPORT VERSES

Don't give chapter and verse—that's too confusing

God is good. His nature is love. His purpose in history is to save men, not destroy them. The Bible says: "For God so loved the world, that he gave his only begotten Son, that whosoever believeth in him, should not perish, but have everlasting life." It also teaches that God "will have all men to be saved, and to come unto the knowledge of the truth." One other verse that has made a great impact on my life is this: "The Lord is not slack concerning his promise, as some men count slackness; but is longsuffering to us-ward, not willing that any should perish, but that all should come to repentance."

KEY CONCEPT

God is good

Somehow, most people don't think of God as good. Powerful, yes. But not good. I guess that's because most men don't see God as good and loving; they spend most of their time running from Him. But God is good. That means God wants what is good for me. That is tremendous. Before I was born, God already had a wonderful plan for me.

ILLUSTRATIONS

Don't feel bound to my illustrations

I remember a story in which a young woman was given wrong information about a man. She was told that the man was an enemy agent. Actually, he was a representative of a large insurance company. He tried in every way he knew to meet

80

the woman to inform her that she was the beneficiary of a million-dollar insurance policy. One night she saw him coming toward her down a dark street. She began to run. He chased her relentlessly. Upon reaching the point of exhaustion she became despondent. "All is lost!" What a shock it was when he caught up with her and said, "My dear, I mean you no harm. I have in my briefcase a certified check with your name on it, made out for the sum of one million dollars." How foolish we are to run from a God who is good.

Running from a fortune

Some people believe that God is fiendishly and arbitrarily selecting who will go to eaven and who will go to hell. They picture God as similar to the officer standing before the cattle cars that pulled up to the Nazi concentration camp—the officer who gleefully pointed some people to the gas chambers and some to the labor camps. But God is not like that. The Bible says it is not God's will that anyone be separated from Him and perish. His desire is for "all men to be saved and come to the knowledge of the truth."

God is not a fiend

Our precious heavenly Father has almost limitless patience with us. He sees us on the wrong road, the road that leads to death. Picture a speeding car going down a dark road toward a gully where a bridge had been washed out. Then picture concerned people who understand the situation as they see the car approaching. They hurriedly push rocks in the road, chop down trees, and set up roadblocks. They try to place every possible obstacle in the road to destruction. That's what God is doing. He is placing obstacle after obstacle in front of sinners who are racing toward destruction.

Divine obstacles

One of the most amazing verses in the Bible is found in Matthew 25:41. "Depart from me, ye cursed, into everlasting fire, prepared for the devil and his angels." God never intended for men to perish in hell. It was created for Satan and his demons. If men go there, it will be their choice—not God's. Yet men seem to love their wanderings down the path that leads to destruction. I'm glad God graciously places roadblocks in our way!

Consider this verse

BRIDGE

"God is good. He doesn't want anyone to perish. Yet look around you. Men are perishing. There are signs of death everywhere. Why do you suppose that is?" Because

Learn your bridges thoroughly

81

2. THE BIBLE TEACHES THAT ALL MEN ARE SINNERS

Support Verses: Isaiah 53:6; Jeremiah 17:9; Romans 3:10; Romans 3:23

Key concept: "Me first" impulse that leads to *rebellion*

Illustrations: a. My relative: "I'm not a sinner."
b. My children when they were babies
c. The world we live in

Bridge: "Now the frightening thing is that the Bible teaches us that there is a terrible consequence awaiting those who sin."

SUPPORT VERSES

The Bible confirms what human history reveals and what our own hearts admit. All men are sinners. This is how the Bible puts it: "For all have sinned, and come short of the glory of God." That's quite a statement, isn't it? There are no exceptions. No man is perfect. None of us is what God intended him to be. The Bible also says: "As it is written, there is none righteous, no, not one." But perhaps the most convincing verse of all is found in the book of Jeremiah, where we find: "The heart is deceitful above all things, and desperately wicked: who can know it?" We hear many romantic ideas about our hearts. But the Bible says that at the very core of our being there is something wrong.

KEY CONCEPT

The *me first* principle

Six hundred years before the birth of Christ, the prophet Isaiah pictured clearly just what is wrong with mankind. He wrote, "All we like sheep have gone astray; we have turned every one to his own way" (Isaiah 53:6). That's the definition of sin: everyone insisting on having his own way. There is a strong impulse in the natural man that insists on putting himself first. We say to everyone else, "Stay out of my way. I'm coming through."

That attitude is reflected in the way men feel about God. Their hearts cry, "God, stay out of my life! I can be happier by myself! Just leave me alone. I'm going to have it my way. I know what makes me happy. I'll give you an hour on Sunday, but the rest of the week is mine. No one is going to tell me how to run my life." Thus, we shake the angry fist of rebellion in God's face.

82

I have a relative who is amused when I tell her that all men are sinners. To her, a sinner is someone who has committed a felony. Therefore, she looks at me and says, "Oh, I'm not a sinner." What she is saying is that she has never committed murder, or armed robbery, or aggravated assault. But she cannot comprehend that sin is much deeper than that. It is an attitude of heart that the unsaved man cannot cure. It is the lust to be independent.

I remember when my kids were little. Our oldest, Ricky, loved to crawl up to the cupboard where his mother kept all our breakfast cereal. She would say, "Ricky, no—no! Stay out of the cupboard." But as soon as she wasn't looking, Ricky had Cheerios and Wheaties all over the kitchen floor! No one was going to stop him from doing what he wanted to do. He was going to have his own way.

That is the drama which is unfolding in our world today. Everybody is telling everyone else, "I'm going to do it my way! I want my own way!" Professional athletes want their own way. They demand five-year contracts for millions of dollars. Team owners, however, want their way. Labor unions want more money. Business wants bigger profits. Teachers want to rule their classrooms. So do the students. Israel wants her own way; the Arabs want theirs. Everyone in a traffic jam wants his own way. Petty dictators in the third world want their own way. All the wars that have ever been fought have involved a power that wanted its own way. There is an irresistible impulse in the natural man that says, "Me first. I'm going to get what I want, and no one is going to stop me!" That basic selfishness is the root of sin—and we all share it.

BRIDGE

"The frightening thing is that the Bible teaches us that there is a terrible consequence for those who sin. Do you know what it is?"

3. THE PENALTY FOR MAN'S SIN IS DEATH

Support verses: Ezekiel 18:4; Romans 6:23
Key concept: Separation
Illustrations: a. Adam and Eve
             b. Three kinds of death
Bridge: "Mr. Brown, I have just told you about a horrible possibility. It is the most frightful

"I'm not a sinner!"

What's happening in the world?

Sin has both present consequences and an awful, ultimate consequence

83

reality that a human mind can conceive. But I am thankful that I do not have to stop here. I have told you the bad news; now it is my joy to be able to tell you the good news. That's what *gospel* means—good news."

SUPPORT VERSES

Let's review what we have been saying for a moment. God is good. He does not want anyone to perish, but millions are perishing. Why? Because all men are sinners, and the penalty for a man's sin is death. The Bible says that God pays men a wage—a salary—for their behavior. It's just as if we were punching in on a divine time clock. Listen carefully now to the wages that the Bible says are due sinners: "For the wages of sin is death; but the gift of God is eternal life through Jesus Christ our Lord." It also says, "The soul that sinneth, it shall die."

KEY CONCEPT

Have you ever wondered what death is really all about? I have. I'm studying this issue in the Scriptures. I have discovered a definition for *death*. *Death* means separation. Whenever death takes place, separation takes place. When men sin, a holy God must separate Himself from them. When men sin against each other, they erect barriers between themselves. When a husband is unfaithful to his wife, his relationship with her dies. It is a law of the universe.

ILLUSTRATIONS

Do you remember how death came into the universe? In the second chapter of Genesis, God said to Adam: "Of every tree of the garden thou mayest freely eat: but of the tree of the knowledge of good and evil, thou shalt not eat of it: for in the day that thou eatest thereof thou shalt surely die." The rest of the story is painfully familiar. Adam and Eve ate the forbidden fruit. "But," you say, "there did not die that day." Oh yes, they did. From that very moment, their bodies began to deteriorate. Their cells began to die. They were locked into processes that would inexorably lead to physical death. But far more than that happened.

When they ate the fruit, they became conscious of guilt. They no longer wanted God to see them. They fled from His presence. A barrier to their fellowship with God had been erected. They died

Review frequently to stress the logic of your development

Death is separation

Adam and Eve reveal the biblical concept of death

spiritually. Their lives had become separate from the life of God.

They fled from God. But God also separated Himself from sinful man. God reminded them that there were two special trees in the Garden of Eden: the tree of the knowledge of good and evil (representing man's choice) and the tree of life (representing God's presence and His salvation). When Adam and Eve sinned, they had to leave the garden. Why? Because their sin became a barrier between them and God. They could no longer be where the tree of life was. In other words, their sin separated them from the presence and salvation of God.

The Bible speaks of the three kinds of death. Do you know what they are?

1. The first is *physical death*. This is what happens when a man's soul and spirit are separated from his body. It happens when a man's heart stops beating. They put his body under six feet of dirt, but his soul never enters that grave. It has become dissociated from the body. All men are going to die physically some day. (Quote Hebrews 9:27.)

Physical death

2. Second is *spiritual death*. This identifies the condition that takes place when a man's spirit is separated from the Spirit of God. The book of Ephesians says, "And you hath he quickened [made alive], who were dead in trespasses and sins." That's amazing! People living—but dead. The pulse is normal, the temperature is ninety-eight point six degrees, the arms and legs move—but the people are dead. You see, when a person is separated from God, he is unable to understand why he is unfulfilled, unhappy. We were created to be joined to the life of God. When we are separated from Him, we cannot live a life that truly satisfies.

Spiritual death (see also Isaiah 59:2)

3. Third is the *second death*. The second death is the most fearful of all human possibilities. It is mentioned twice in the book of Revelation. This is what it means: when a person who has chosen to live independently from God dies, that separation becomes eternal. The Bible clearly teaches that that individual will be separated forever in hell from the life of God. Hell was created for Satan and his angels. God doesn't want anyone to perish. All our lives, He is placing roadblock after roadblock across the path that leads to hell.

Be sure you are familiar with 2 Thessalonians 1:8-9 and Revelation 20:14

"I have just told you about a horrible possibility. It is the most repulsive reality that a human mind can conceive. But I am so thankful that I do not have to stop here. I have told you the bad news; now it is my joy to be able to tell you the good news. That's what *gospel* means—good news."

Emphasize the contrast

4. JESUS CHRIST, GOD'S WONDERFUL SON, DIED ON CALVARY'S CROSS TO PAY THE FULL PENALTY FOR MAN'S SIN

Support verses: Romans 5:8; 2 Corinthians 5:21; 1 Peter 1:18-19; 1 Peter 2:24; 1 Peter 3:18

Key concept: Christ our Substitute

Illustrations: a. Criminal court judge who says, "Guilty," but offers his life in place of the criminal's
b. Soldiering during the Civil War

Bridge: "When I was sixteen, I learned the most important fact of my life. I learned that it is not enough to have some facts about Christ and His death swimming around in our minds somewhere. Almost all religious people in America say that they believe in Christ and His death on the cross, but they still don't have peace with God. Do you know what makes the difference?"

SUPPORT VERSES

We have mentioned that God is holy. Because of His holiness, sin must be banished from His presence. But He is also loving—He doesn't want anyone to perish. That is the dilemma. Theoretically, there are three things that a Holy God could do with respect to sinful men. *First,* He could act in *holiness* and judge men by banishing everyone to hell. But his very nature is love, and He does not want anyone to perish. *Second,* He could act in *love* and ignore men's sins. But his very nature is holiness, and if God ignored sin He would not be God. *Third,* He could send a Substitute to pay the full penalty for men's sins.

The divine dilemma

That is exactly what God did. The Bible says, "God commendeth [or proves, or demonstrates] his love towards us, in that, while we were yet sinners, Christ died for us." That little word "for"

86

means "in our place." He died in our stead—instead of us.

The Bible goes on to say, "He hath made him to be sin for us, who knew no sin; that we might be made the righteousness of God in him." This verse in Corinthians speaks of *the great exchange*. Christ exchanged His righteousness for our sins so that when we place our trust in Him we can exchange our sins for His righteousness.

The great exchange

Scripture is very specific about the work of Christ and what it means to us. Peter said about Christ, "Who his own self bare our sins in his own body on the tree, that we, being dead to sins, should live unto righteousness." Twice in that verse, the writer speaks of Christ's taking our sins upon Himself. Peter continues by saying, "For Christ also hath once suffered [*that is,* died] for sins, the just for the unjust, that he might bring us to God."

Perhaps my favorite verses that deal with how Christ paid for our sins are 1 Peter 1:18 and 19: "Forasmuch as ye know that ye were not redeemed with corruptible things, as silver and gold . . . but with the precious blood of Christ, as of a lamb without blemish and without spot."

KEY CONCEPT

Christ became our Substitute. He died in my place. That is why He is often referred to as the Lamb of God. John the Baptist saw Jesus and exclaimed, "Behold, the Lamb of God, which taketh away the sin of the world!" (John 1:29). The Jewish people who were with John understood the meaning of this metaphor. Every year the high priest of the Jews would take the blood of an unblemished lamb and go into the Holy of Holies (the place that represented God's literal presence) and offer the blood for the sins of the Jewish nation. God has decreed that without the shedding of blood there can be no forgiveness of sins (Hebrews 9:22).

The principle of a perfect Substitute is the core of the gospel

But the fascinating thing is this: The blood of the lamb never really paid for sin. It was just a symbol pointing to Jesus Christ, who was one day going to come as the Lamb of God to take away the sins of the world. What is even more wonderful is that God was pleased with Christ's ultimate sacrifice. The demands of holiness have been satisfied perfectly. He is at liberty to forgive the sins of men who trust Him.

The blood of Christ

87

A judge substitutes for his son

One day in a court in England a young man stood before a judge, who also happened to be his father. The son had been accused of a serious crime. The evidence was presented. The father listened intently. Finally, he concluded: "He is guilty." But then he did an astounding thing. He got up from the bench and stood by the boy, and said: "But I will bear the sentence for him. I will pay his debt." That is substitution. God is not letting our sins go unpunished. He is not closing his eyes to them. They have been placed upon Christ. He bore them at Calvary. He died with our sins upon Him.

One man substitutes for another in the Civil War

During the Civil War, a man with enough wealth who feared military service could pay another man literally to take his place in the ranks. Imagine a soldier, with your number, fighting your battle! Imagine, further, that months later you were informed of his death in combat. You are alive because another took your place in death. That is what Christ did for us.

BRIDGE

It's not enough to have a vague understanding

We must act (choose to rely) upon what we know

"When I was sixteen, I learned the most important fact of my life. I learned that it is not enough to have some facts about Christ and His death swimming around in our minds somewhere. Almost all religious people in America say that they believe in Christ and in His death on the cross, but they don't have peace with God. Do you know what makes the difference?"

5. EVERY PERSON MUST EXERCISE SAVING FAITH. THAT IS, HE MUST CLAIM BY PERSONAL CHOICE AND RELY EXCLUSIVELY UPON THE WORK OF CHRIST ON THE CROSS TO BE SUFFICIENT PAYMENT FOR HIS SIN

Support verses: John 1:12; Romans 3:24-25; Romans 4:20-21; Hebrews 6:18

Key concepts: Choice and Trust

Illustrations: a. Window shopping
b. Drowning man
c. Sitting in a chair
d. Receiving a gift

Bridge: "I believe that I can summarize everything I have been saying in three sentences. First, all men are sinners, and sin separates from God. Second, Calvary is God's only provision for man's sin. And third, we must each exercise saving faith, which is claimed by personal choice and relying exclusively upon Christ's work on the cross to be sufficient payment for our sin."

SUPPORT VERSES

Romans teaches us wonderful truths about salvation. We are justified freely by God's grace (we cannot earn salvation), and God is satisfied with us when we put our faith in Christ's shed blood as payment for our sins. But we must make a choice. The Bible says, "As many as received him, to them gave he power to become the sons of God, even to them that believe on his name." Faith is active. It is seizing for ourselves what God has made available.

KEY CONCEPTS

Saving faith has two parts.

1. First, it is *claiming by personal choice*: A person always chooses to put his faith in something. No one will find himself in heaven against his will. Nor will anyone ever be able to say, "I'm a Christian, but I sure didn't want to be. My parents made me do it." Saving faith is active. There is a quality about faith that honors man's unique capacity to determine his own destiny. Man is truly remarkable. He has been given the right to choose. For two thousand years, Christians of all backgrounds and cultures and ages have shared this common denominator: they have freely chosen to place their trust in Christ's saving work.

A choice

Hebrews 6:18 is a verse that aptly explains faith in terms of claiming by choice. It says, "We . . . have a strong consolation, who have fled for refuge to lay hold upon the hope set before us." There are three issues here. First, there is the consciousness of need and danger. The writer speaks of the need to flee from something horrible. That corresponds to a sinner's becoming aware of the penalty of his sin—the possibility of being visited upon by the wrath of a holy God. Second, there is the perception of a shelter, a perfect provision, which is instantly available. That corresponds to the eternal life God promises those who come to Him through the blood of Christ. It is held out to sinners. It is offered freely, without cost. Third, there is the conscious decision to grasp this provision for oneself. The verse says we are to lay hold of the hope set before us. That is the choice of saving faith.

The best way to explain choice: "to lay hold upon" (Hebrews 6:18)

My wife and I love to window shop. That's reasonable. I'm a preacher, and we don't have any money. We go to the big shopping centers that surround Chicago, and we stare. It's great fun. But imagine standing before the most beautiful store of all and looking at a sign in the window that says: "Anything that you want in this store is yours—without charge—if you will come in and claim it."

Now, that kind of sign would surprise anyone. But let's double our surprises. Suppose you stand by that sign, invisibly, and see thousands of people read it, laugh, and go on their way. No one believes it. "It's not logical," they say. "You can't have something for nothing." People walk by. Then someone says, "Hey, I know the owner of this store. He means exactly what he says!" Five minutes later, he walks out with twenty new suits and eight mink coats!

God asks men to believe

God says to men today, "I have paid for your salvation with the precious blood of My own Son. I offer it to you without charge. All I ask you to do is to claim it by conscious choice for yourself." Men laugh at God's way of saving people because they believe that it is not logical. They feel much more comfortable making a deal with God,

Men try to make deals

so they say, "Lord, if you will save me I will purchase that salvation with full surrender, perfect devotion, and a life of selfless service. I will give up smoking and drinking. I will start going to church." Men feel more comfortable making deals with God. God grieves at each attempt. He sees men mock His grace and reject His mercy. They will not grasp by choice that which He freely offers to whoever will believe.

God asks us to make a choice. Our volition is involved in saving faith. Imagine you are drowning and about to go down for the last time. Suddenly, miracle of miracles, a boat appears on the horizon. It speeds to your aid. A strong, knowledgeable seaman flings a life preserver in your

Choosing is not a work

direction. Providentially, it lands inches away from your head. All you must do to be rescued is place your arm around the life preserver. This act has no merit. Rather, it is the only response of hopeless need. God sees us sinking. He offers us His Son. Again, the issue is uncomplicated but profound: we must take hold of His provision. He has done everything. He asks only that we claim His salvation.

90

2. The second part of saving faith is *relying exclusively upon Christ's work on the cross.* We have noted that saving faith involves our *will.* It also involves our *trust.* Trusting, or believing, is our ability to rely exclusively upon the promise of God. Two verses from Romans 4 illustrate this quality better than any other verses in the Bible. They speak of Abraham, who was told by God that he was going to become a father when he was one hundred years old and his wife was ninety. Impossible! It couldn't be done! Absurd! Medical science laughed in disbelief. Who would Abraham believe—science or God? He chose to believe in a God whose Word had never failed him. Abraham "staggered not at the promise of God through unbelief; but was strong in faith, giving glory to God; and being fully persuaded that, what he [God] had promised, he was able also to perform" (Romans 4:20-21).

That was faith. Abraham, before he saw any evidence of pregnancy in Sarah, was already thanking God for his new son! He was relying upon the fact that God doesn't say things that He doesn't mean. "Abraham believed God, and it was counted unto him for righteousness" (Romans 4:3).

ILLUSTRATIONS

Faith, actually, is like sitting in a chair. You look for a chair that is well built or has been tested by personal experience. Then you take the step of faith—you sit down on it. That's what "relying exclusively upon" means—sitting down in the promise of God. God says to us, "I promise you that if you come to Me through faith in Christ's blood—that is, believing that My Son, Jesus Christ, died on Calvary's cross to pay for your sins in full—I will give you eternal life." Faith is grasping that promise for ourselves. It is taking the objective, historical fact of Christ's crucifixion and applying its merit to our sin problem. God promises you eternal life if you rest your hope in Calvary's sufficiency. *He asks you to recline in his promise.*

If a man were to hold out to you a hundred-dollar bill and say: "It's yours if you take it," you would have a decision to make. You would ask yourself, "Can I rely on his word?" If the answer is yes, you would enthusiastically reach out your hand and claim that gift for yourself.

Note carefully that God asks us to rely exclusively upon Christ's work. His provision cannot be

Saving faith involves both will and trust

Abraham's faith

Reclining in God's promise

91

The acid test: "exclusively"

mixed with human performance. God is very jealous about this. Christ did it. We are to believe it. That settles it forever. When we find ourselves placing our hope for eternity in Calvary plus something, we miss everything. The gospel makes exclusive claims. A man is saved by faith alone, or he is not saved at all. Good works grow out of saving faith; they do not in any way contribute to our salvation. The verse that often comes to mind when I consider saving faith as "relying exclusively upon" is Romans 4:5: "But to him that worketh not, but believeth on him that justifieth the ungodly, his faith is counted for righteousness."

BRIDGE

"I believe that I can summarize everything I have been saying in three sentences. First, All men are sinners, and sin separates from God. Second, Calvary is God's only provision for man's sin. And third, we must each exercise saving faith, which is claiming by personal choice and relying exclusively upon Christ's work on the cross to be sufficient payment for my sin.

"May I ask you a question? Do the things that I have been saying really make sense to you?"

REVIEW OF CHAPTER 7
A COMPREHENSIVE APPROACH
TO PRESENTING THE GOSPEL

PHASE TWO: PRESENTING THE FIVE BASIC TRUTHS
OF THE GOSPEL

We have found it extremely valuable to be able to sharpen our focus about the gospel by crystallizing it into five basic propositions, each succeeding one built upon the former. This basic outline must be enhanced by your own personality, illustrations, and so forth. The presentation of the gospel is not a magic formula—it is a systematic, logical, passionate setting forth of saving facts. It may take five minutes or five hours to present this message in such a way that it produces conviction and understanding.

It may be helpful if you think of your presentation of the gospel in terms of a body: the *outline* of the gospel is the skeleton, the *Scripture verses* that support this outline are the muscle, and the clear *illustrations* of those facts are the flesh that helps to make rather abstract truths practical and vivid.

1. God is good, a God of love, who does not want anyone to perish.
   a. God is good—stress this. His nature is to cherish His creation.
   b. Some people think God delights in "predestining" people to hell out of fiendish pleasure (like a Nazi concentration camp officer). Nothing could be further from the truth.
   c. The Bible clearly teaches that *it is God's will for everyone to be saved* (1 Timothy 2:4). If people are lost, it is not God's fault; rather, it is their own fault. Hell was not created for men (Matthew 25:41).
   d. In fact, God lovingly puts obstacles in our path to destruction.
   e. Yet men are perishing.
   (Bridge: Look around—signs of death everywhere! Why? Because . . .)
2. The Bible teaches that all men are sinners.
   a. Many people are confused about what it means to be a sinner.
      (1) Some think sinners are only those who do horrible things.
      (2) My aunt said to me: "Oh, I'm not a sinner."
   b. But the Bible teaches that sin is the natural impulse of all men to say: "God, stay out of my life." It is living in accordance with the "me first" impulse (Isaiah 53:6).
      (1) It is an attitude of rebellion that is characterized by the motto: "I want to do it my way. So, God, leave me alone. I can do it better by myself."
      (2) It is a fierce, proud determination to do just what I please.
   c. The important thing is to understand that all men have this attitude of rebellion. Yes, all men are sinners (Romans 3:23). Do you agree with me?
   (Bridge: Now, the frightful thing is that the Bible teaches that there is a terrible consequence for those who sin.)

3. The penalty for man's sin is death.
   a. Do you know what death means? It means separation.
   b. Adam and Eve lived in a garden that had a tree of life (representing salvation). When they sinned they were cast out of the garden (that is, separated from the life of God).
   c. Because God is perfectly holy, sin must be cast out of His presence (2 Thessalonians 1:9).
   d. The Bible says that there are three different kinds of death (or separation):
      (1) Physical death: the separation of my soul from my body (Hebrews 9:27)
      (2) Spiritual death: the separation of my life from the life of God (Ephesians 2:1)
      (3) Second death: eternal separation of the sinner from the presence of God forever in a place called hell (Revelation 20:14).
   e. God loves us, but we are sinners who deserve His banishment.

   (Bridge: This is the worst thought anyone could probably think! But now I want to tell you the most wonderful truth in the Bible.)

4. Jesus Christ, God's wonderful Son, died on Calvary's cross to pay the full penalty for man's sin.
   a. Jesus Christ was God. He did not have to die, because He never sinned. Why, then, did he die?
   b. He died as our *Substitute*. That means, He died in our place. He died the death that we deserve.
   c. When Christ died on the cross, therefore, He took all our sins upon Himself. He paid for *every* one of them. He paid for the sins of the world! He became "the Lamb of God, which taketh away the sin of the world" (John 1:29; *see also* 1 Peter 1:18-19).
   d. That is the meaning of the word *redemption*. Jesus Christ "bought us back" from slavery to sin by paying for sin with His own precious blood. God's demand for perfect holiness was satisfied at Calvary.
   e. The resurrection of Christ is God's great sign that He is satisfied with the price paid for sin. Hence, the penalty for your sin has already been paid.
   f. But it is not enough to have a few of these facts swimming around in your mind.

   (Bridge: Most religious people in America believe in Christ and His death on the cross. Yet they have no peace. Why?)

5. Each person must claim by personal choice and rely exclusively upon Christ's work on the cross as sufficient payment for his sin.
   a. Saving faith involves our *will* and our *trust*.
   b. We must *choose* to believe. No one will be in heaven against his will. There comes a moment of time when a person says: "This is for me! I take it! I choose Christ to be my Savior." (Hebrews 6:18). I "lay hold upon" God's promise.
   c. *Trust* is also involved. Faith is the ability to rely on what God says. This is not a feeling or an experience. God says: "My Son died for your sins. The work is finished. Trust in His shed blood and I promise you eternal life" (Romans 4:20-21).

A BRIEF OUTLINE OF THE GOSPEL

"I believe that *everything* the Bible says about salvation can be crystallized into five great truths. May I tell them to you?"

1. *"God is good, a God of love, who does not want anyone to perish."*

   Key Concept: The goodness of God. All of history is God's gracious attempt to keep us from traveling down the road that leads to destruction.

   Bridge: "But men are perishing; why? Because . . ."

2. *"All men are sinners."*

   Key Concept: Sin is living according to the "me first" impulse that has as its root *rebellion* against God. ("God, I want to do it my way. Stay out of my life!")

   Bridge: "The Bible says that sin carries with it a fearful consequence . . ."

3. *"The penalty for man's sin is death."*

   Key Concept: Death means separation. The Bible speaks of three kinds of death:
   a. Physical death: Separation of body and soul.
   b. Spiritual death: Separation of my life from the life of God.
   c. Second death: Separation forever from the presence of God, in hell.

   Bridge: "I've just told you terrible news. Please let me now tell you the good news. Do you know that *gospel* means 'good news'?"

4. *"Jesus Christ, God's wonderful Son, died on Calvary's cross to pay the penalty for man's sin."*

   Key Concept: Christ became our *Substitute.* He took our sin upon Himself so that we could claim His righteousness. He died in my place.

   Bridge: "Many people say that they have always believed in Jesus Christ, yet they have no peace concerning eternity. Do you know why that is?"

5. *"We must exercise saving faith. Saving faith is claiming by personal choice and relying exclusively upon Christ's work on the cross to be sufficient payment for my sin."*

   Key Concept: Saving faith is willful trust.
   1. It involves *choice*: laying hold, personally, upon God's promise.
   2. It involves *trust*: this is our responsibility to "sit down in," or rely upon, the sufficiency of Christ's blood to pay for our sin.

ASSIGNMENTS

1. Memorize the five points of the gospel outline.
2. Tell your evangelism partner the five points and the Scripture verses you have memorized that support each proposition.
3. Develop your own illustrations for each of the five truths or modify the ones in this chapter to fit your own experience.

QUESTIONS FOR DISCUSSION

1. We have suggested that our five-point presentation is simply a vehicle to make the three crucial issues of salvation logical. What would be lacking if we eliminated any of these five truths? Discuss each of the five points individually.
2. Do you understand the doctrine of repentance? How is this doctrine (as presented in this chapter) different from the way it is presented by so many evangelists today?
3. Explain what is meant by salvation by grace alone.
4. What are God's three options in dealing with sinners?
5. Explain why we must be careful to point out that saving faith has two ingredients.
6. Make a list of each bridge in our presentation. Do they really work? Are they natural?

PRAYER

Pray that God will give you insight into the message of the gospel and that you will feel comfortable telling it to others.

8

A Comprehensive Approach to Presenting the Gospel

Phase Three: Leading to the Point of Decision

INTRODUCTION

Since the days of D. L. Moody, pressing for a decision has been a familiar part of evangelicalism. The concept of coming to a point where one claims Christ's provision for himself is quite in keeping with our definition of faith. We have just concluded a study of what saving faith means, and at its very heart is the concept of volition, or free choice.

Although the concept of a decision is biblical, it scares some of our laymen for one reason and scares some of us preachers for quite another. Let's take a look at two attitudes that ought to be avoided.

1. First is an *inability to "tie the knot."* Many of the longtime Christians who have taken our training complain that their attempts to evangelize in the past have been frustrating. They have told a thousand facts about Christ to someone, but the listener still isn't saved. This week a woman came up to me after one of our workshops and said, "Pastor, I've been talking to a woman about Christ and have told her everything I could think of. She nods in agreement with me, but from the things she says I don't believe she's saved. Where do I go from here?"

Have you ever said that to yourself when you were squarely in the middle of a witnessing opportunity? I have an observation to make. It is easier for people to talk in the third person about relationships with Christ than it is to confront someone openly—that is, talk to an individual

If faith involves will, will involves a decision

Two problems relating to decisions:

1. Inability to tie the knot

97

2. Gaining decisions at any cost

My experiences with easy decisions but no conviction or understanding

It takes time for people to see—be willing to come back as often as necessary

about *his* spiritual need. Until we can do that with confidence, our witness will be less than satisfying. We will always come to the point of asking, "Where do I go from here?" It is the fear of confronting a person directly about his need that scares most laymen.

2. A second attitude to be avoided is that of *gaining decisions at any cost.* To me, this attitude is even more frightful. It is caused by overzealous evangelists who are commonly referred to as "scalp hunters" or "trophy counters." For them, soul-winning is big business. The numbers of decisions they record is the mark of their spiritual success. Again, I say that this mentality frightens me. In extreme cases it can lead to the heresy of allowing the end to justify the means.

I have seen the fruit of this kind of evangelism. Perhaps I should say I have seen the lack of fruit. When I was first saved, I went through a stage of my life during which I wanted a surefire method of soul-winning. I used this little booklet or that little pamphlet and told three or four steps to salvation to people and then asked them to read the prayer on the back page. Presto! A convert! But one by one those people who were now supposed to be my brothers in Christ started to avoid me. I made them uncomfortable. They felt that they were living a lie around me. What went wrong? In time it became obvious. Those people found it easier to "roll with the punches" of my gospel presentation than to say no. People were making "decisions" without understanding, without Holy Spirit conviction, without desire.

I was so ashamed of myself that I vowed never again to ask a person to read a printed prayer in order to get saved. I would never again ask a person to pray after me the words that I prayed. In fact, I would never put words about salvation into a man's mouth. Now I feel much more comfortable. I want to be absolutely honest about presenting the facts of the gospel: yes, even the facts that offend. But then I want to prepare a climate in which a person can be equally free to respond in honesty. My task: to make things clear. His task: to make a free choice.

Nor would I ever rush an inquirer. It takes time for the Holy Spirit to do His precious work. It takes time for a heart to be prepared. I would rather make four visits to the same home than rush a person into an insincere decision that first night. Remember, *success in evangelism must be measured by our faithfulness in sharing a life-*

changing message, not by how many people make a decision for Christ in our presence.

Many people have listened to my gospel presentation and then said something like this: "It sounds wonderful, but it is all so new to me. I just need some time to think these things through." That is a perfectly legitimate response. When I hear it, I respond by giving them a book to read, pointing them to a study of the gospel of John, and asking them if I may visit them again another week. Sometimes I will say, "Wow, I can see that you are right on the verge of the biggest decision of your life! Will you do me a favor? When you see it—when you claim Christ's blood for yourself—will you give me a call on the telephone and share the good news with me?" Probably a dozen people have done just that in recent years.

Before we study this matter of decision making in detail, I want to relate one more story that illustrates the folly of pressing for decisions for decisions' sake apart from understanding, or Holy Spirit conviction, or genuine desire.

Not too many years ago I was invited to attend a prayer breakfast in the small town in which I was pastoring. It was a rare opportunity for me because the breakfast was sponsored by the mainline denominational churches of our town. A millionaire from Texas was going to be the featured speaker. He was going to talk about how Christ had changed his life. More than two hundred fifty of the leading businessmen of our county attended. From that standpoint it was a smashing success. Then the millionaire began to speak. First he told some jokes. Next he described how he had become so successful. Next he told the men some lessons he had learned about love. He told us all that we could learn to love by faith. Finally, he asked the men to bow their heads. He urged us to turn over the corner of the card under our plates if we would like to invite Christ into our lives.

Afterward, the tabulation was made. Scores had turned over the corners of their cards. Men were declaring that revival had come to Hamilton County! But there was no revival. To the best of my knowledge, not one of the men who turned over the corner of his card was genuinely converted. But how could they have been? All three of the great, central issues of Christianity had been ignored. There was no mention of men being lost in their sins. No mention of the pre-

"Give me a call!"

It is not difficult to get people to make a decision

99

cious blood of Christ. No explanation of what constitutes saving faith.

The choice

That became a turning point in my ministry. I saw that it was easy to get people to make decisions. I had to make a choice. Would I gear my ministry toward causing thousands to make decisions based on a watered down gospel, or would I settle for far fewer decisions based on the unashamed exposition of the gospel of grace? That is the choice you must make today. I pray that you will make your choice on the sole basis of preparing people to live forever—to face eternity.

TWO HELPFUL QUESTIONS

You have completed your gospel presentation, which was the subject of our last chapter. You have summarized the gospel by sharing the three great issues: *first,* man's problem (all men are sinners, and sin separates from God); *second,* God's solution (Calvary is God's only provision for man's sin); and *third,* our responsibility (we must exercise saving faith; saving faith is claiming by personal choice and relying exclusively upon Christ's work on the cross to be sufficient payment for my sin).

It is now time. This is the moment for which all men were born. Generalizations in the third person must be abandoned. You are now pressing an individual to confront his own spiritual need. It may well be that he has never been asked to do this before. You are not apologetic. You are not pushy. You are vitally concerned. The bridge between your gospel presentation and the actual decision comes in the form of two questions:

Two questions that set the stage for a decision

1. First is the *general question:* "Do the things that I have been telling you about really make sense?" This is an absolutely necessary question. You have been doing most of the talking. You have no idea what has been going on in the mind of the other person. You must find out. Be prepared for anything. If the individual answers *yes* with confidence, you are ready to ask the second question. If, however, the answer is *no* or says that he is not sure, you must ask the person exactly what confuses him. Be very patient. You have plenty of time. You are equipping a soul to face eternity. Never look as though you are bored or irritated by a person's confusion. This is the point in your presentation when you encourage your listener to tell you his thoughts. This is his opportunity to ask questions or tell you his opinions on anything you have said.

1. "Does this make sense?"

When you understand his problem, answer it as precisely as you can. Then review the three great issues. Now repeat the question: "Now do the things I have been telling you about really make sense?" If the answer is yes, you are ready to ask the crucial question.

2. That second and crucial question is the *specific question:* "Tell me, Mr. Brown. Is there any reason you can think of that would prevent you from placing your trust in the Lord Jesus Christ and His shed blood, thus receiving Him as your own personal Savior right now?"

2. "What's stopping you?"

If he answers negatively, you are at liberty to proceed with the issues of decision. But there are two other answers frequently given. The first is, "I have always believed the things you are telling me. I think I've always been a Christian." If you hear that response, you must remind your listener of his answer to your question about what he would say if God should ask him why He should let him into heaven. Perhaps your reply will be something like this:

"Mr. Brown, I hope you will forgive my directness, but I have never met a born-again Christian who would answer the question I asked you earlier the way you did. I asked you how you would answer God if He were to ask you, 'Why should I let you into My heaven?' and you said, 'I have always tried to live a godly life and do the best I can.' Do you remember? No one who understands Christ's work on the cross would have given your answer."

This is the moment of greatest tension. The person you are talking to may think you are calling him a liar. You are simply trying to force him to face an inconsistency. Many people will face it squarely. They will see that what they mistook for lifelong beliefs is only mental assent to vague facts about Christ. They will admit that this is not enough because it has not brought peace to their hearts. They are now ready to go on.

The most common answer to the question, "Is there any reason you can think of that would prevent you from placing your trust in the Lord Jesus Christ and His shed blood, and thus receiving Him as your own personal Savior right now?" is: "Yes, there is!" Good. A person has been honest with you. You appreciate that. Now you must discover the reason. Out of many possible reasons, let me suggest five:

Reasons why some hesitate:

101

1. "It'll alienate me from my family."

1. "This could alienate me from my family."

One young lady said that her parents would kick her out of their home if she became a Christian. It is a genuine possibility. Here are some of the ways this reason can be handled:

"In my own experience, I have found that since I have become a Christian I have more love for my family than ever before. And the interesting thing is that I think they love me more than ever before also."

"Yes, it could. But some questions in life are even bigger than your family. There comes a time when the only important factor in making a decision is: Am I doing the right thing? This is the mark of maturity."

"Most parents want the best for their children. They have sacrificed a great deal for our happiness. Don't you believe that your parents would be pleased if they saw in you a change that produced great joy, peace, and inner contentment?"

"Our Lord Himself forced us to face this possibility when He said that in order to be His disciple, other things, such as vocation, family, and personal interests, must not come before Him as the most important thing in our lives."

2. "It didn't work before."

2. "I've tried it already and it didn't work."

Now we are reaping the results of someone else's poor technique in evangelism. So many millions have made some kind of religious decision that never had any effect. Some very religious people say that they have tried to take Christ into their lives every day. This can be very frustrating. We must have answers.

"You don't try to believe. Faith is an intelligent stand based on rational, objective facts. I'm so glad that I don't have to tell you to try to believe. I ask you only to look at what happened in history. You must not try to believe a myth. But as you look into the Bible and see what Christ did, you become aware that this is true; and because you are convinced it is true, you claim it."

"The fact that you tried something that didn't work is probably the evidence that you never really understood the facts of the gospel and therefore could not have believed."

"I don't try to believe in George Washington. I accept his existence on the basis of the reliable testimony of history. Remember, becoming a Christian is not a mystical experience. God tells us to claim for ourselves the benefits of something that actually happened.

"Many people have made outward decisions but were not really sincere. Is it possible that you were one of those who just went through the motions?"

3. *"I just don't feel right about this. I feel sort of uneasy."*

This reason for delaying one's decision is real. Do you remember how you felt when you first heard the gospel? If you were in a public meeting, your heart was pounding so loudly that you were sure that you were disturbing the saints sitting next to you. Consider these suggestions:

"Satan will do all in his power to make you put off this decision."

"It is never easy to come to the place in your life where you reckon for the first time with your spiritual need. It is rather shattering to discover that you are lost apart from faith in Christ."

"You have a perfect right to feel uneasy right now. When two people stand before a preacher in the act of marriage and recite their vows, they, too, are uneasy, because they are entering into something that has lifelong consequences. The decision you are being asked to make will determine your eternal destiny."

4. *"You are absolutely right, but I just don't want to see my life changed."*

"Salvation doesn't depend on a changed life but on Christ's finished work. You cannot put the cart before the horse. All the Lord asks you to do is recognize your spiritual need and claim His gracious provision for meeting that need."

"What I think you are really saying is that you are not interested. If that is your position, then salvation is not for you. But remember this: Every man is going to have to give an account of his life to the great God of the universe."

"I don't believe you. I have met thousands of people who tried to appear happy and content on the outside, but on the inside they were miserable. Could that be true of you?"

5. *"I'm just not sure."*

Be very patient and understanding with this person. His uncertainty is probably very real. The Holy Spirit must be given time to accomplish His work. Ask the person to tell you the nature of his uncertainty. If it is rational and can be put into words, you will probably be able to settle the problem on the spot. But some uncertainties

3. "I'm nervous, uneasy."

4. "I don't want to change."

5. "I'm not sure."

103

cannot be answered that way. If you see no hope for immediate resolution of the problem, suggest that you get together again. Give him literature to read and ask him to read the gospel of John. Ask him to write down his thoughts as he reads.

THE MOMENT OF DECISION

At a point in time a person becomes a Christian. He is indwelt by the Holy Spirit of God. He is born again. That moment is known to God. However, it is not known to the evangelist, and in many cases ardent Christians cannot pinpoint the hour in which they were saved.

Knowing this, we must avoid the tendency to try to predict the minute in which a person is saved. We press for a decision in three straightforward questions. We then have several options for prayer. Later, we discuss the matter of assurance. Somehow, as these issues are covered, people are wonderfully saved. Again, this does not mean that a person is saved as soon as he gives an affirmative answer to a question. *He is saved only when he rests his hope of eternity on Christ's finished work.* Our responsibility is to assist him in seeing this truth and claiming it for himself. Therefore, a decision is not a spooky thing. It is the reasonable response of an enlightened mind.

Let's go back to our last question: "Is there any reason you can think of that would prevent you from putting your trust in the Lord Jesus Christ and His shed blood, thus receiving Him as your own personal Savior right now?" "No, there isn't." It is time to confront the person with the gigantic issues of eternity:

HE MUST RECOGNIZE THAT HE IS A LOST SINNER

"Do you take your place — right now — before God as a lost, hell-deserving sinner, absolutely powerless to lift a finger to save yourself?" "Yes I do."

"Wonderful! For most human beings, that is the hardest fact of life to admit."

HE MUST RECOGNIZE THAT JESUS CHRIST DIED ON THE CROSS FOR HIS SINS — AS HIS SUBSTITUTE — IN ORDER TO BECOME HIS SAVIOR

"Do you believe that Jesus Christ is the Son of God who shed His precious blood at Calvary to pay the full penalty for your sin?"

"Yes, I certainly do."

(You might have to explain that a person's decision is made as he is confronted with three questions)

104

"I'm very glad! But I must now ask you the most important question of all."

"Will you, right now, claim by faith alone the free offer of eternal life that God promises to anyone who will place his hope in the finished work of Christ?"

"This is all so new to me! But I think I understand. Yes. I claim this gift of salvation right now."

THE PLACE OF PRAYER IN THE DECISION-MAKING PROCESS

Prayer is simply one person verbalizing his thoughts to another person—a divine Person. We must be careful to point out the place of prayer in the decision-making process, for many people are led to believe that they are saved through their prayer rather than through their faith.

We offer two options concerning the use of prayer in the decision-making process. First, if its function is to clarify the decision just made, it is best offered at this moment in your presentation. Second, if it is felt that a person will think that he has to pray in order to be saved, it is better to go over the matter of assurance first, and when he is confident that he is saved forever, have a time of prayer just to say "thank you" to God.

Many of us believe that prayer brings clarity of thought to the person who has already made his decision by giving affirmative answers to the above questions. Thus, we urge a person to pray as soon as those answers are given. The very ability to verbalize the issues of decision will bring confidence and assurance.

Never pray a written prayer with your prospect. Never ask him to repeat your phrases after you. If you do, you will lose the precious opportunity to see if he really understands what is happening. *He must pray his own prayer. He must speak his own thoughts.* Only God knows for sure if the prospect is sincere. But you must not fail to let the prospect use his own words.

It is perfectly in order to suggest to the person, before he prays, the things that he ought to include in his prayer. Ask him to express these thoughts to God *in his own words:* I know that I am a sinner. I believe that Jesus Christ died to take away my sins. Right now I am claiming by faith the gift of eternal life, which God has promised to all who believe in Christ's sacrifice for their

Many pray "to receive Christ," thus leaving the issue open-ended and failing completely to gain assurance

Do not use prayer until the decision has been made

Prayer is a good way for a person to say thank you for what he now knows that he has

sin. I thank God for my salvation.

THE MATTER OF ASSURANCE

After you have confronted the seeker with the three questions of decision, you may choose to ask him to pray (you should then pray after him), or you may direct his thoughts to the matter of assurance. Turn in your Bible to John 6:47. It ought to be underlined for emphasis. Ask your listener to read the verse out loud. Ask him to read it again. Now tell him that you want him to read it once more, but after he does you are going to ask him some questions about the meaning of the verse:

"Verily, verily, I say unto you, He that believeth on me hath everlasting life."

"Mr. Brown, who made that statement?"

"Jesus Christ."

"That's right, and the Lord Jesus Christ does not lie. We can trust His word. Christ promises us something in this verse. Do you see what it is?"

"Eternal life."

"Again, you're right. As you look at this verse, you will note that Christ's promise has only one condition. Do you see what it is?"

"Believing in Him."

"Have you believed on the Lord Jesus Christ tonight? That is, have you put your trust in what He did for you on the cross?"

"Yes."

"Then if you were to die tonight, where would you spend eternity?"

"Why, in heaven."

"Praise the Lord! Mr. Brown, I'm very happy for you! Welcome to the family of God!"

You are now ready to leave, but before you do, you want to leave your name and phone number so that the new convert can call you if any questions arise. Give him some hints on beginning the Christian life. Ask him to begin to read the gospel of John. Make a date to visit him again just to answer the flood of questions that are now going to engulf his mind. But by all means, don't leave until you have done these two things.

First, tell him that when a person is saved he is saved forever. Tell him that he will still have ups and downs; he will still sin. After all, he is just a new spiritual baby. Satan will try to discourage him. But he will never have to be saved again. When Christ saves us, when we are born again, we are the proud possessors of eternal life. Nothing or no one can separate us from Christ. We are

Memorize these questions, which focus on John 6:47

Before you leave:

Give your name and phone number

Suggest another meeting

Tell him about the believer's security

joined to Him in an indissoluble union. *See* John 10:28-29 and Romans 8:38-39.

Second, ask him to tell someone what has just happened to him. This is most important. Tell him to talk to a Christian he knows (everybody seems to know one!), or his spouse, or his best friend. This will psychologically reinforce his decision and also give him great satisfaction.

Encourage him to tell someone what has just happened to him

REVIEW OF CHAPTER 8
A COMPREHENSIVE APPROACH
TO PRESENTING THE GOSPEL

PHASE THREE: LEADING TO THE POINT OF DECISION

1. One's decision *must* be made on the basis of *understanding.* Take great pains to be sure that the one with whom you are talking clearly understands the issue.
   a. Summarize the gospel by reviewing the *three great issues.*
      (1) Man's problem: All men are sinners, and sin separates from God.
      (2) God's solution: Calvary (Christ's shed blood) is God's only provision for man's sin.
      (3) Man's responsibility: Exercise *saving faith.* Saving faith is claiming by personal choice and relying *exclusively* upon Christ's work on the cross to be sufficient payment for our sin.
2. After you have comprehensively shared the gospel, you must compassionately ask the person you are talking with two questions that will encourage him to trust Christ.
   a. *General question:* "Do the things that I have just been telling you really make sense?" (If no, go back as far in your presentation as necessary. If yes, ask the specific question.)
      (1) This is the time for you to become a listener. This is the time for the prospect to show his questions and confusions. In fact, encourage him to do so.
      (2) Stop here if you are not persuaded that the person is under conviction.
   b. *Specific question:* "Is there any reason you can think of that would prevent you from placing your trust in the Lord Jesus Christ as your personal Savior right now?"
3. Possible answers: If the answer is : "Yes, there is."
   a. "This could alienate me from my family."
      (1) My experience—more love from and more love for my family than ever before.
      (2) Yes, it could. But some questions in life are even bigger than your family.
      (3) Most parents want the best for their children. They want them to have a purpose.
      (4) Christ insisted that He must come before family.
   b. "I've tried it already and it didn't work." (*Many* have made some sort of blind religious commitment already.) Be sure to have a good answer for this response.
      (1) You don't *try* to believe. Faith is an intelligent stand based on objective facts. An honest exposure to the Word of God makes faith a very reasonable thing.
      (2) The fact that "it didn't work" is proof that you never understood or really believed. It is because Christianity is true (and I know it!) that I claim it for myself.
      (3) I don't try to believe in George Washington; I accept his existence on the basis of the reliable testimony of history.
   c. "I just don't feel right about this. I feel sort of uneasy."
      (1) Satan will do all in his power to make you put off this decision.

(2) You ought to feel uneasy right now, for this is a decision that determines your eternal destiny.

d. "You're absolutely right, but I just don't want to see my life changed."
   (1) Salvation doesn't depend on a changed life—rather it depends on faith in Calvary. What you are really saying is that you are not interested.
   (2) If you are not interested, salvation is not for you. But remember this: Every man is going to have to give an account of his life to the great God of the universe.

e. "I'm just not sure."
   (1) Be very patient with this man—if his uncertainty is real. The Holy Spirit must be given time to accomplish His work.
   (2) Ask the person to tell you the nature of his uncertainty. If there is no enlightenment, suggest that you get together again.

4. The answer he gives may surprise you. Before you presented the gospel, he admitted that his hope of heaven was good works. Now he answers, "I think I have always believed that."
   a. You now point out his inconsistency (without calling him a liar!). "Mr. Brown, after talking to hundreds of people about their hope of heaven, I have discovered that they reveal what they are *really* depending on when I ask them the question about why God should let them into His heaven. Could this be true with you?"

5. If the answer to the question in 2.b. of this outline is no, *then solemnly* tell the person you are talking to about the three points below, which deal with *the core of one's decision.*
   a. *He must recognize that he is a lost sinner.* "Do you take your place before a holy God as a lost sinner—absolutely incapable of lifting a finger to save yourself (through religious exercises or moral reformation)?"
   b. *He must recognize that Jesus Christ is his Savior, his Substitute.* "Do you believe that Jesus Christ, God's perfect Son, shed His precious blood on Calvary to pay the full penalty for your sin?"
   c. He must *claim salvation.* "Will you *right now* claim by faith the free offer of eternal life that God promises to all who place their hope in Christ's work?"

6. The place of prayer in decision making.
   a. Prayer is simply one person verbalizing his thoughts to a divine Person.
   b. Prayer doesn't save anyone. Only faith does.
   c. *Never* pray a written prayer. *Never* have someone pray phrase by phrase after you. Rather, offer suggestions about what the person should pray and then ask him to tell his thoughts to God *in his own words.*
      (1) Tell God that you know you are a sinner.
      (2) Tell Him that you believe that Christ died for your sins.
      (3) Tell Him that right now you are trusting in a finished work and have received the free gift of eternal life promised to all who believe.
      (4) Thank Him.
   d. If a person says that he doesn't feel comfortable praying out loud, honor his feelings. We have forced ourselves to believe that a person cannot be saved without praying. That is simply not the case.

7. The matter of assurance.
   a. Open your Bible to John 6:47. Ask the person to read it out loud.

(1) "Who made this promise?"
  "Jesus Christ."
(2) "What did He promise?"
  "Everlasting Life."
(3) "On what condition?"
  "Believing."

b. "Have you believed on the Lord tonight? That is, have you put your trust in Him?"

"Yes."

"Then let me ask you this question: If you were to die tonight—right now—where would you spend eternity?"

"Why, in heaven."

"Who said so?"

"Jesus Christ."

"Praise the Lord, welcome to the family of God!"

8. Never leave the home without telling the person two more things.
   a. When a person is saved, *he is saved forever.* "You will never have to get saved again. Yes, you will battle with sin, but sins can never again separate you from salvation." (See John 10:28-29 and Romans 8:38-39.)
   b. Encourage your convert to tell a trusted friend or loved one what has happened before the day is over.

ASSIGNMENTS

1. Master answers to the two questions that lead to a decision.
2. Memorize the three questions of decision. Know them perfectly.
3. Memorize John 6:47.

QUESTIONS FOR DISCUSSION

1. Why has it been difficult for you to bring people to the point of decision?
2. At what point in the decision-making process do you feel most comfortable about praying?
3. How do you know when you are becoming too pushy?
4. What does a person have to know in order to make an intelligent decision?
5. What are the extremes to avoid in bringing people to Christ?
6. What other reasons would prevent a person from claiming Christ as Savior?
7. Why is it wrong to tell a person that he is saved?

PRAYER

Ask God to give you a great desire to see people come to the point of decision. Ask Him to give you wisdom to know when to press for a decision and when to wait for the Holy Spirit to accomplish His work.

A COMPREHENSIVE SUMMARY OF PRESENTING THE GOSPEL

PHASE ONE: FROM THE FIRST MINUTE OF CONVERSATION
TO THE DISCERNMENT OF A PERSON'S NEED

Key Issue	Basic Presentation	Bridge
Objective: To win a hearing for the gospel from a total stranger.	1. *Introduction:* a. Address him by name: "Hello, Mr. Brown."	"May we take a few minutes of your time to talk to you about Bobby's Sunday school class?"

110

	b. State your name immediately. c. Identify your church unapologetically. d. Clarify your purpose. e. Take the initiative of inviting yourself in.	
Objective: To put the other person at ease and become comfortable yourself.	2. *His secular life:* a. Talk about the things about which you believe he will feel most comfortable talking. b. Look for hints of special interests: hobbies, etc.	"What church did you attend back in Wisconsin?"
Look for hints about his spiritual condition.	3. *His religious life:* a. Listen positively. b. Do not try to encourage criticism.	"By the way, how did Bobby begin to attend our Sunday school?"
Stress the purpose of our activities.	4. *The aspect of our church that affects him:* a. Stress the aspect he knows about. 1. Sunday school. 2. Youth clubs. 3. Bus routes. b. Ask how he feels about this ministry. c. Tell him the purpose of this ministry.	"We have a Sunday school to teach boys and girls how they can have eternal and abundant life. I certainly have not always had that kind of life."
Objective: To whet his appetite for more.	5. *My personal testimony:* a. What life was like before I trusted Christ. b. Exactly what it was that made the difference. c. How Christ has changed my life since I have become a Christian.	"Wow, I'm talking about myself. Do you mind if I ask you a question?"
Make sure that he understands his hope of heaven.	6. *Two important questions:* a. (General): "Have you come to the place in your own spiritual life where you know for certain that if you were to die tonight you would go to heaven?" b. (Specific): "Suppose you were to die today and stand before God, and He should say to you, 'Why should I let you into my heaven?' What would your answer be?"	"Now I know I have good news for you!"

Key Issue	Basic Presentation	Bridge
God is *good*. He wants all men to be saved.	1. *God is good, a God of love, who does not want anyone to perish.* a. Some people think of God in terms of a ruthless Nazi exterminator. b. Actually, God is lovingly putting obstacles and roadblocks in our path toward destruction.	"Look around you; there are signs of death everywhere. Men are perishing. Why?"
Sin is living according to the "me first" impulse. It is *rebellion* against God. ("Stay out of my life.")	2. *All men are sinners.* a. Many think of sinners as those who have committed a felony. b. Actually, sin is: 1. Living according to the "me first" impulse. 2. It is *rebellion* against God. ("I'll give you an hour on Sunday, but the rest of the week is mine.") 3. It is the outward fruit of a selfish life (selfish acts). c. We are not sinners because we sin, we sin because we are sinners.	"The Bible says that sin carries with it fearful consequences."
Death is *separation*. The Bible speaks of three kinds of death.	3. *The penalty for man's sin is death.* a. Death literally means separation. b. A holy God must separate Himself from sinful men. He must banish sinners from His presence. c. There are three kinds of death in the Bible: 1. Physical—separation of body and soul. 2. Spiritual—separation of my life from the life of God. 3. Second Death—separation from God forever in hell.	"This is the most horrible thought of which a human can conceive. but now I want to tell you some wonderful 'good news.'"
Christ is our *Substitute*. He died in our place.	4. *Jesus Christ, God's wonderful Son, died on Calvary to pay the full penalty for man's sin.*	"It's not enough to have facts about Christ swimming around in your head. Most religious people

112

Key Issue	Basic Presentation	Response of Listener
	a. Jesus Christ was God. He did not have sins of His own to die for. Then why did He die? b. Christ died as our *Substitute.* We deserved sin's penalty: death. Christ died for us. He paid for our sins. c. The resurrection of Christ is God's great sign that He is satisfied with the price for sin. Hence, the penalty for *your* sins has already been paid.	in America know these facts but have no peace."
Saving faith involves *choice* and *trust.*	5. *We must exercise saving faith, which is claiming by personal choice and relying exclusively upon Christ's work on the cross to be sufficient payment for our sin.* a. Faith involves choice: We must lay hold of God's provision. b. Faith involves trust: Trust is the ability to "sit down" in God's promise.	Review the three crucial issues: "Do the things I have been saying really make sense to you?"

PHASE THREE: LEADING TO THE POINT OF DECISION

Key Issue	Basic Presentation	Response of Listener
Now he must clearly understand these issues.	1. *Review the three crucial issues:* a. Man's problem: All men are sinners, and sin separates us from God. b. God's solution: Calvary is God's only provision for sin. c. Our responsibility: Exercise saving faith—claim by personal choice and rely exclusively upon Christ's work on the cross to be sufficient payment for our sin.	
You cannot run ahead of one's *understanding.* If there is no clear understanding, a decision is absolutely meaningless.	2. *Two questions on decision:* a. (General): "Do the things I have been telling you really make sense?" b. (Specific): "Is there any reason you can think of that would prevent you from putting your trust in the Lord Jesus Christ and His shed blood, thus receiving	"Yes, they really do."

	Him as your own personal Savior?"	"Yes, I just don't think it will work for me. I've tried it before."
	3. *Deal carefully with the reason:* a. "You don't try to believe . . ." etc. b. If his problem has been cleared up, ask the specific question again.	"Now I think I am ready."
The decision is rational, not mystical. It is willful trust in the work of Christ.	4. *The decision itself:* a. He must recognize that he is a sinner. "Do you take your place before God as a lost, hell-deserving sinner, absolutely powerless to lift a finger to save yourself?" b. He must recognize that Jesus Christ died for his sins. "Do you believe that Jesus Christ is the Son of God who shed His blood at Calvary to pay the full penalty for your sin?" c. He must *claim salvation.* "Will you *right now* claim by faith alone the free offer of eternal life that God promises to anyone who will place his hope in the finished work of Christ?"	 "Yes, I do." "Yes." "Yes, I will."
Prayer can be a delightful resource to confirm a decision.	5. *The place of prayer:* a. It is simply talking to God, telling Him out loud what has just been done. b. Never read a prayer or ask someone to pray after you, phrase by phrase. c. Instruct the person about what thoughts to include.	

This is crucial. Go over this matter until enlightenment comes.	6. *The matter of assurance:*
	 a. Have him read John 6:47
	   1. "Who said it?"
	   2. "What did He promise?"
	   3. "On what sole condition?"
	 b. "Have you put your trust in Him—and on what He did for you?"
	 c. "Now, if you were to die tonight, where would you spend eternity?"
		
		"Jesus Christ."
		
		"Eternal life."
		
		"Believing in Him."
		
		"Yes."
		
		"Why, in heaven!"

114

9

Avoiding Confusing Terminology in Evangelism

We have systematically introduced you to a practical method for witnessing. That is the positive purpose of this manual. It is wonderful to know how to lead men to Christ. A person is never the same again after he has the joy of leading a man or a woman to Christ. I trust that you will soon have that thrill.

But there is another purpose for writing. I am burdened about what I see happening in much of the evangelical community. There is much *talk* of gospel but very little gospel being preached. How can that be? Many people are talking about Christ in vague language that misses the key issues altogether.

Recently our young adults went to a roller skating party. At the intermission, a football coach from a nearby high school was introduced to give a devotional thought. He was kind and sincere and had a real burden to see teens become Christians, but the substance of his evangelistic invitation was: "Make Christ a part of your life." That is not the gospel. Many people from what is commonly called Christendom are trying to make Christ a part of their lives, but with little success.

Many years ago, I took a course in evangelism, and the professor said that the irreducible core of evangelism is "giving all you know of yourself to all you know about Jesus Christ." Again, I protest. That is not the gospel.

One more incident is noteworthy. We visited another evangelical gathering, and a former beauty queen, who was not only very lovely but also very charming, was talking about her faith. The closest that she got to evangelism was to

Have you used these clichés?

115

quote a very popular phrase: "Commit your life to Christ." I know I run the risk of being labeled picky, but that also is not the gospel. In fact, that phrase is as popular with liberal theologians as with conservative. I believe that I could walk into any Rotary Club, YMCA, Boy Scout meeting, or garden club affair in the country and talk about committing our lives to Christ, and no one would object. Everyone would think it was a great idea. Everyone would smile at me, and after the meeting the people would all slap me on the back and say that they enjoyed my speech.

The gospel centers on Jesus' work on the cross

I want more than that from life. I want to see folks saved. In order for that to be accomplished, they must hear the gospel. There is no other way. The gospel centers on what Jesus has done on Calvary's cross. The cross is the bridge that alone can unite men to a holy God.

We live in a day when everyone is being influenced by the mass media. Fundamental-evangelicals are no exception. We are all barraged with different religious terminology. Radios give us the views of preachers from coast to coast. Now, one by one, Christian television stations are appearing. Some of the people in our church test my messages not by the standard of Scripture but by the standard of their favorite Christian celebrity.

One of the problems of living in a media-oriented society is facing the temptation to dilute the offensive aspects of the Christian faith in order to appeal to ever greater audiences. The urge, indeed the pressure, to do this is almost irresistible. Christians in high places gain an audience by inviting newly converted rock stars, celebrities, and professional athletes to give their testimonies. I don't blame the celebrities for what they say. But I do find fault with a system that is more concerned about mass appeal than teaching the truth.

It is dangerous to dilute the gospel for a broader appeal

It is our conviction that much of the common evangelical language used to promote evangelism is confusing at best and heretical at worst. There is such a thing as poetic license in which phrases are chosen for emotional stimulation rather than intellectual enlightenment. But we are talking about *evangelism*. This is not the arena in which to be shoddy and imprecise. Evangelism is like heart surgery. It demands our total concentration. It requires maximum precision. How can we trifle with human lives?

How will we know when our terminology is

116

adequate? We will know when we have succeeded in persuading men that they must face a single issue: *Will they claim as their hope of eternal life the historic, space-time sacrifice of Christ, who died for the sins of the world?* This is an objective message.

We know that our terminology is faulty if it

1. Fails to provide us with an adequate basis for our faith;

2. Implies that something other than exercising faith on our part is necessary in order to be saved;

3. Causes the inquirer to depend upon his subjective, emotional response for his assurance;

4. Fails to declare that the issue in believing is: "Where is your hope? Upon what are you *depending?*";

5. Deals too lightly with sin and its consequences—or fails to convey to the listener the horror of his lostness.

The gospel concerns the death and resurrection of Jesus Christ, "who was delivered [to the cross] for our offences, and was raised again for our justification" (Romans 4:25). His death is the *ground* of our hope. His resurrection is the *certainty* of our hope. Today this message is being confused with a gooey emotionalism that asks a man to imagine that he must do, feel, experience, or surrender in order to find peace with God. When we add anything to the age-old formula— "faith in Christ's blood"—we lose everything.

Paul, in Philippians 1:15-18, did not object to people's preaching the right message for the wrong reasons. In fact, he rejoiced. But that same Paul became furious when he heard that the Galatians were falling prey to the wrong message. It is important to recognize that the Galatian heretics were not trying to deny Christ. They loved to talk about Christ. Their error was to insist that something other than simply believing—in their case, circumcision—must be done by the seeker of Christ.

The Book of Galatians was written to combat that error. Paul says, "I marvel that ye are so soon removed from him that called you into the grace of Christ unto another gospel" (Galatians 1:6). He continues, "If ye be circumcised [if you depend on circumcision to help save you], Christ shall profit you nothing" (Galatians 5:2). It is the humbling fact of being able to contribute nothing to our salvation that Paul calls "the offence of the cross" (Galatians 5:11). The natural man despises

The goal of terminology is evangelism

Ask yourself constantly: "Am I providing my listener with an adequate basis for faith?"

Paul's argument

117

this truth. He would add something—anything—that could dilute grace. There is in each of us an almost irresistible urge to *add something more* to the New Testament message: "Whosoever believeth in him should not perish" (John 3:16).

Lance B. Latham has captured magnificently the central issue: "Ask any religious person: 'Do you believe in Jesus Christ?' and he will say, 'Of course!' Is this man therefore saved? The real question is, 'Where is your hope?' Are you *depending* upon Christ alone and what He has done at Calvary, or is your hope in penances performed, masses, baptisms, and so forth? That is not faith in Christ and His work; it is faith in you and *in your own works*. None of these can save. A lifetime of tears, vows, faithfulness to a church, and daily self-denial could not bring peace to a hungry heart.

"One large religious movement declares that 'to believe' means to turn the direction of your life over to Christ. This is fatally *wrong*. This is again presenting 'works' as the way of salvation in another subtle form. No! Faith in Christ sees Him at Calvary paying in *full* for all my sins—past, present, and future. Good works—that is, new direction of our lives—*never causes, but always springs from* our resting as undeserving sinners in Christ's work at Calvary. Hebrews 6:18 well expresses the essence of saving faith: 'Who have *fled for refuge to lay hold* upon the hope set before us.' Faith is being personally satisfied in what Christ, who is God, God's unique Son, did for us when hanging on the cross of Calvary."

WRONG DIRECTIONS

Clichés to avoid:

Let's look now at some of the suggestions given to those desiring to be saved. Let's see how they can be misleading. I know that many dedicated Christians use these expressions from time to time. We don't want to appear petty. All of us want to discover the best ways to make the gospel clear. Sometimes that clarity comes by examining confusing clichés.

1. "Give your heart to Christ."

1. The first misleading suggestion we will look at is *"Give your heart to Christ."* It sounds positively romantic. And, in a sense, there is affection involved in Christianity. We love Christ because He first loved us. But we are not saved by falling in love with Jesus. We are saved by believing in His sacrifice for us. Moreover, salvation is not my gift to God; it is His gift to me. Let us be sure that

Listen to Lance Latham

118

we understand *exactly* who it is who holds out empty hands toward heaven and who places in those hands the priceless gift of eternal life.

We ask the question: On what Scripture does such an invitation rest? We find in Proverbs 23:26, "My son, give me thine heart." But surely that is not an adequate justification for an invitation so generally given. Moreover, that verse is addressed to "my son" (a relationship that is already established). There are two dangers in telling someone that he can be saved by giving his heart to Christ. First, how would anyone really be able to know when he had given it? After all, millions of religionists are trying to give their lives to God *every* day. They are plagued with uncertainty. There is no adequate ground for knowing when you have succeeded. Second, this appeal lacks an adequate basis for salvation. In such an invitation there is no thought of encouraging a person to rely on Calvary's sufficiency. Apart from Calvary, there is no basis for lifelong confidence that in spite of your ups and downs you are acceptable to God.

2. A second misleading suggestion is *"You must forsake all your sins."* I'm absolutely astounded by this appeal. Once I heard a British preacher dogmatically say that one must forsake all his sins in order to get saved. It was not ten minutes later that he was making an appeal to Christians, saying, "Now, brothers, I know there is sin in your lives also!" Incredible! First he told us that one can be saved by forsaking his sins; then he told *the saved* to forsake their sins! Such contradiction.

I'm glad that the Bible tells me that there are only two kinds of people in the world: sinners and saved sinners. If people had to promise that they would live nobly and godly every moment of their Christian lives in order to qualify for salvation, no one would qualify. How can the unregenerate make such a promise? Romans 8:7 says, "The carnal mind is enmity against God: for it is not subject to the law of God, neither indeed can be." No, God accepts us as we are. He justifies the ungodly. "But to him that worketh not, but believeth on him that justifieth the ungodly, his faith is counted for righteousness" (Romans 4:5). Afterward, as new creations in Christ, we will perform good works (Ephesians 2:10).

3. *"You must pray: 'God be merciful to me a sinner'"* is another misleading suggestion. You have perhaps heard this invitation used in rescue

2. "You must forsake all your sins."

3. "You must pray: 'God be merciful to me a sinner.'"

4. "You must surrender all to Christ."

missions. Doubtless many have been saved in spite of this kind of decision-making technique. Then comes the follow-up quotation: "Save me for Jesus' sake." People who say this believe that Jesus fits into the picture somewhere—but where?

Imagine a poor wretched fellow praying this prayer. He goes away from the meeting with a genuine sense of relief. He really wants God's mercy. But in the succeeding days he becomes soberingly aware of his failures and he begins to wonder, *Why should a holy God ever be merciful to the likes of me?...Why?...Why?...* Soon his optimism has faded into the old gloom. He has no basis upon which to claim God's mercy.

Actually, as this prayer was offered in Luke 18:13, its meaning to the publican was clear. He was asking that God be "mercy-seated" toward him. He was asking for grace from a God who was propitiated (satisfied by the payment of a blood sacrifice). Here, assuredly, is adequate grounds for peace. He was coming to God on a solid basis.

4. A fourth misleading statement is *"You must surrender all to Christ."* The great preacher and Bible teacher, William R. Newell, used to say earnestly: "To preach full surrender to an unsaved man as the way of salvation will just make a hateful Pharisee out of him." How true. The natural man wants to be told that he must do something in order to be saved. His mind has been trained to believe you do not get something for nothing. But even more than that, his pride does not want to accept grace. Men don't want to be obliged to God. They want to pay as they go. Yet, as a man begins to implement the life of surrender, he sees that it is more than he bargained for. Finally, he says, "It's hopeless."

Dr. Harry Ironside, formerly the pastor of Moody Memorial Church in Chicago, wrote in his tract *Another Gospel* that "when anyone comes promising salvation to those 'who make a full surrender' of all that they have to God, and who 'pay the price of salvation,' he is preaching another Gospel, for the price was paid on Calvary's cross and the work that saves is finished. It was Christ Jesus who made the full surrender when He yielded His life on Calvary that saves us, not our surrender in any way to Him."

Romans 6:1 is very enlightening in this regard. Paul anticipates a hypothetical question as he asks: "What shall we say then? Shall we continue in sin, that grace may abound?" It is true that grace changes a person who truly understands its wonder. In Titus 2:11-12, Paul said that "the grace of God that bringeth salvation hath appeared to all men, teaching us that, denying ungodliness and worldly lusts, we should live soberly, righteously, and godly, in this present world." But the point is that you know you are preaching grace when someone says to you, "You mean to say that I can go out and kill somebody and still be saved?" Praise the Lord, Christians don't kill people, but they could, and still go to heaven! David did.

If our preaching is so conditional, so fraught with qualifications and regulations that no one could ever misunderstand us and conclude: "What shall we say then? Shall we continue in sin, that grace may abound?" We have not preached the good news of God's grace.

The climactic exhortation that begins the practical section of the book of Romans ("I beseech you therefore, brethren, by the mercies of God, that ye present your bodies a living sacrifice" [Romans 12:1]), is often used to support "I surrender all" salvation. But it is obviously written to brethren—those already saved. Moreover, the basis of the appeal is "the mercies of God." Those mercies have been Paul's subject all through the book of Romans. The mercies (or graces) that motivate one to surrender his life in service to Christ are all the wonderful possessions and privileges that he enjoys only because he believes the gospel and is thus seen by God as being "in Christ." This is not a small issue. When the attempt is made to foist this passage upon unbelievers as a way of salvation, God is robbed of the great victory that grace and grace alone can win.

Yet there is a surrender that people make at the moment of conversion. It is a surrender in the way we think. We say to God, in effect, "God I capitulate. You win. I thought I could save myself through morality and religion. What a fool I have been. Now I see clearly that I am powerless to solve my own sin problem. I give up. Calvary is my only hope."

5. A fifth misleading statement is *"You must make Jesus Christ the Lord of your life."* The basis of this dangerous direction is Romans 10:9, "If thou shalt confess with thy mouth the Lord Jesus, and shalt believe in thine heart that God hath raised him from the dead, thou shalt be saved." Proponents are quick to point out that a

5. "You must make Jesus Christ the Lord of your life."

121

more literal rendering of the text would be, "If thou shalt confess Jesus as Lord." They thus make their case, "You must make Jesus Christ the Lord of your life in order to be saved." Another variation of this theme is that you must put Christ on the throne of your life.

But that is not the point of the verse at all. It is simply saying that no one can be saved who does not recognize who Jesus Christ is. Jesus Christ is God incarnate. Very God of very God: Surely we must see that Jesus Christ is the Son of God or we will perish. Jesus Christ Himself said, "Ye shall die in your sins: for if ye believe not that I am he, ye shall die in your sins" (John 8:24). This is vastly different from making Him the Lord of your life—in other words, promising Him perfect obedience for the rest of your life. When we make this kind of appeal, we are preaching works righteousness. There is no good news here. The miracle of the gospel is, of course, that as we understand *His mercies* and *His graciousness* to sinners, and our exalted position in Christ, we will choose heartily to make Christ Lord. But it will flow from a heart of love and appreciation.

6. "You must open the door of your heart."

6. Finally, a sixth misleading statement is *"You must open the door of your heart. You must receive Jesus Christ."* If we would qualify this form of invitation by explaining that what we must receive is the provision that Christ has made for us at Calvary, this becomes a very appropriate form of invitation. But we are rightly afraid of any invitation that focuses upon the person of Christ and ignores the work of Christ. The Presbyterian Shorter Catechism expresses this proper kind of receiving very ably: "Faith in Jesus Christ is a saving grace, whereby we receive and rest upon him alone for salvation, as he is offered to us in the gospel" (Christ died for our sins).

You may conclude that we are sticklers over words. That is not the case. We simply realize that only the gospel saves. You dare not pass over the blood shed at Calvary and merely receive Christ. "Without shedding of blood is no remission [of sins]" (Hebrews 9:22).

Permit me to summarize the issue of how to avoid using confusing terminology. If you will follow these few guidelines, you will see people gain assurance of their salvation. Yes, it is true that you may not see as many people make outward decisions; the results you do see, however, will last.

(There is one cliché that I don't mind at all: "Bill has just *trusted Christ* as his Savior.")

1. Make sure that your appeal is designed to encourage your listener to claim by choice an ob-

jective message that deals with a great event outside of himself in the real world of space-time history.

2. Insist that the issue is not how a person feels; rather, it is what he believes: what he is relying upon.

3. Never present a message that stresses human performance of any kind as a necessary requirement for the new birth.

4. Emphasize what happened at Calvary. Never allow yourself to stray too far from this bedrock issue.

5. Never give the impression that certain mechanics must be fulfilled in the decision-making process. The issue is not hand raising, tears, formula prayers, or even prayer in general. The issue is faith in Christ's substitutionary work.

6. Avoid using any pet phrase or terminology that neglects the communication of an adequate basis for saving faith (the work of Christ) or that implies that we must do more than see our need and claim by faith God's provision.

7. Do not be romantic about the matter of salvation. The decision must be based on factual reality, not heated passion. Tears may flow—they often do—but one is not saved by crying. Joy results from, but does not cause, Christianity. Be aware of the mind set of your listener. His tendency will be to try to feel saved and to try to act saved in order to convince himself that he *is* saved. That is backward. Only as he sees the rational basis for his Christian faith, only as he believes the gospel, will he be able to feel and act like a new creation in Christ.

The tendency of many: to try to feel "saved"

Look at the following article written by Lance B. Latham which recently appeared in the *Awana Signal* magazine. In just a few paragraphs, it catches the beauty and simplicity of the gospel of grace.

An article by Lance Latham

The Gospel brings a wonderful announcement. At infinite sacrifice, the penalty for all the world's sins—the sins of you and me—has been paid in full at Calvary. "Behold the Lamb of God, which taketh away the sin of the world" (John 1:29). "He is the propitiation for our sins: and not for ours only, but also for the sins of the whole world" (I John 2:2). Every provision has been made for our salvation from sin.

But what must we do to be saved—to receive this great salvation? It is not enough merely to accept the great truths of the Bible. God must first show us through His Word our tragic need to be saved from sin. We are ungodly (Romans

123

4:5), and we are sinners; we have sinned. One sin would bar us from Heaven forever, let alone the multitude of sins we have committed. We must know our need and recognize that we are helpless to do anything about it. We must realize we are lost. The mere fact that we have accepted certain truths about Christ and His death is not enough. We must "believe on the Lord Jesus Christ." We must find our hope, our relief, in relying on Him as dying for our sins on the cross. We must believe by faith that He took upon Himself the punishment we deserved for our sins. Hebrews 6:18 expresses "saving faith" this way: "Who have fled for refuge to lay hold upon the hope set before us."

And let no man deceive you! We are responsible to accept God's Word about our fearful, lost condition, and then find our hope in Christ's death for us on Calvary! Is this your only hope? Do not place your hope in reform, surrender, or goodness. But as a believing sinner, you qualify for salvation—eternal life. And you are responsible to believe!

Now that you have believed, do you really receive eternal life? Is it really true that you will "never perish," as John 3:16 promises? Or are you on probation?

The answer to these questions is all-important. We proclaim that "whosoever believeth in him [the son of God] should not perish [shall not come into judgment], but have everlasting life." God has made a promise, and He will fulfill it. There are so many passages in the Word of God that reinforce this fundamental truth that God saves us forever when we believe on the Lord Jesus Christ. We shall cite merely one of them where God's exalted purpose for us is clearly defined and outlined, Romans 8:29,30:

> *"For whom he did foreknow, he also did predestinate to be conformed to the image of his Son....Moreover whom he did predestinate, them he also called: and whom he called, them he also justified: and whom he justified, them he also glorified."*

Once I am truly saved, I am in God's glorious production line. I am His workmanship. He may have to chasten me again and again, even bring me to the point of utter despair, death, loss. But the Great Workman accepts His Son's death as full payment for my sin, and the blood of Christ shed on Calvary suffices for all my sins—past, present, future. Moreover, the Holy Spirit of God is faithfully working to accomplish in life that which always accompanies salvation (1 Cor. 1:8-9) and present me "faultless before the presence of his glory with exceeding joy" (Jude 24).

124

There is no other Gospel but that of the glorious grace of God. Let us preach and teach salvation, not probation. We can well cry out with the Apostle Paul, "If God be for us, who can be against us?"

I would like to close this chapter by making a general observation: If we neglect the part of our witness that stresses the *need* for salvation, we will invariably look for the reality, or the "punch," of conversion in conditions that we attach to *obtaining* salvation.

We don't want anyone to miss the fact that there is a difference between Christians and non-Christians, so we force that "difference" to be the commitment of our lives to Jesus Christ. If we would spend more time dealing with the wretchedness of being lost, the horror of our sinfulness, the deep-rootedness of our selfishness—we would not have to attach human requirements to the gospel of grace. Instead, like the jailer of old, people would be asking us, "Sirs, what must I do to be saved?" (Acts 16:30). Then we could let the *good news* be good news indeed. We could share Christ's perfect provision and ask dying men only to claim it—to latch onto it by faith alone. No qualifications or reformations would be necessary.

You ask, "Don't we have to tell men that they must be willing to turn from their sins?" Let me ask you a question: Can you imagine the folly of being in a lifeboat, seeing a man drowning in the ocean, approaching his side, and saying, "I have good news for you! You can come up here with me in the lifeboat and be safe—but you must be willing to come out of the water."

How patently ridiculous! If we have adequately presented the sinner's need, we will not have to insist that he "come out of the water." If the Holy Spirit has convicted a man of his sin, we can say, "I have good news for you!"

Let me repeat this observation: The more we neglect the first part of our presentation (the explanation of sin and its consequences), the more we will feel a need to add "teeth" to our invitation, and we will invariably do it by asking a man to commit his life to Christ. Isn't it ironic that a Christian desires to live completely for Christ simply because he has seen the grace of God in operation? He shouts, "I am the recipient of love, grace, pardon, salvation, riches—that I do not deserve. Hallelujah, what a Savior!"

What produces change?

125

REVIEW OF CHAPTER 9
AVOIDING CONFUSING TERMINOLOGY
IN EVANGELISM

1. What the gospel is not.

    In this day of mass media proliferation, one is constantly barraged with different religious terminology. It is our conviction that much of common evangelical language is confusing at best and heretical at worst. Our desire is to present the gospel with such precision that *the inescapable issue is one's personal faith in the historic, space-time sacrifice of Christ, who died for our sins on the cross of Calvary. This is an objective message.* Today, however, this message is being confused by subjectivism that causes one to imagine that he must do, feel, experience, or surrender—that is, *add something more* to the New Testament message: "Whosoever believeth in him should not perish" (John 3:16).

2. What does it mean to believe?

    Ask any religious person in America, "Do you believe in Jesus Christ," and he will probably say, "Of course!" Is this man therefore saved? The real question is, "Where is your hope?" Are you *depending* upon Christ and what he has done at Calvary alone, or is your hope in penances performed, masses, baptism, and so forth? That is not faith in Christ and His work—that is faith in *your own* works—and therefore it *cannot save.*

    Hebrews 6:18 well expresses saving faith: The saved "have fled for refuge to lay hold upon the hope set before [them]."

    One large movement declares that "to believe" means to turn the direction of your life over to Christ. This is fatally *wrong.* This is again presenting works as the way of salvation in another subtle form. No! Faith in Christ sees Him at Calvary paying in *full* for my sins—past, present, and future. Works—direction of life—spring from our resting as undeserving sinners in Christ's work at Calvary. Faith is being personally satisfied in what Christ, who is God, did for us when on the cross of Calvary.

3. Wrong directions. We feel that certain directions frequently given to those desiring to be saved can be misleading.

    a. *"Give your heart to Christ."*

        To the man on the street in modern America, this phrase connotes romantic involvement. However, one is not saved by falling in love with Jesus, but by believing in Him. Moreover, salvation is not my gift to God, but His gift to me. This also applies to like invitations such as, "Give your life to God" and so forth.

        And, on what Scripture does this invitation rest? We find in Proverbs 23:26, "My son, give me thine heart." Surely there is no justification in this one verse for an invitation so generally given. And, it is addressed to "my son"—an already established relationship. Here, there is no reliance on Calvary set forth.

b. *"Forsake all your sins."*

This means for the sinner to promise to live perfectly from now on. I read in Romans 8:7 that "the carnal mind is enmity against God: for it is not subject to the law of God, neither indeed can be." No! God accepts us as *ungodly—as we are—*when as sinners we trust in Him and His redeeming work on Calvary. Then, once we are justified, we gain a new perspective on sin. Sin robs us of joy, fellowship, and accomplishment. We now have Christ living in us, and we begin to feel about sin the way He does (1 John 4:17*b*).

c. *"God be merciful to me a sinner."*

This is commonly used in rescue missions, and doubtless God saves many in spite of such an incomplete invitation. And do you notice what usually is added?—"And save me for Jesus' sake" doubtless because it is thought that if "Jesus" enters in somewhere, it is the plan of salvation. The Scofield note under Luke 18:13 gives a good teaching about this verse: "merciful" should have been translated "mercy-seated" or "pro-pitiated," for the idea here is not that of mere mercy—a special idea is meant. See Scofield's note.

The problem with this appeal is simply: "Why should a holy God be merciful to me? On what ground can He be merciful?" Apart from the cross, there is no answer.

d. *"Surrender all."*

William R. Newell says, "To preach *full surrender* to an unsaved man as the way of salvation will just make a hateful Pharisee out of him." And, from Dr. Ironside's tract *Another Gospel:* "When anyone comes promising salvation to those 'who make full surrender' of all that they have to God, and who 'pay the price of full salvation,' he is preaching another gospel, for the price was paid on Calvary's cross and the work that saves is finished. It was Christ Jesus who made the full surrender when he yielded His life on Calvary that saves us, not our surrender in any way to Him."

The climactic exhortation in Romans 12:1, "I beseech you therefore, brethren, by the mercies of God, that ye present your bodies a living sacrifice," is addressed to brethren—those already saved. And the basis for that appeal is "the mercies of God"—the wonderful possessions we have in Christ, possessions presented in the previous chapters of Romans. Applying this to the salvation of unbelievers robs God of the great victory that grace, and grace alone, can win. And, even if I gave my body to be burned and have not love, my sacrifice would profit me nothing.

e. *"Make Jesus your Lord."*

This is just another variation of the "surrender all' invitation. Surely, we must recognize who He *is* or we will die in our sins (John 8:24). But this is vastly different from making Him the Lord of your life—in other words, promising to obey Him the rest of your life. This latter is again preaching "works." His mercies, with all His graciousness to us, *will lead* us to make Him Lord out of a heart of love and appreciation of Him.

Those who propose this way of salvation, we feel, change the obvious meaning of Romans 10:9: "If thou shalt confess with thy mouth the Lord Jesus." This verse cannot be made to say, "make Him Lord of your life." The change of one word would clear up the difficulty. The issue is: "If thou shalt confess with thy mouth that Jesus Christ is God."

No one can be saved who does not confess this!

    f. *"Receive Jesus Christ."*

        If we would state this as it appears in the Presbyterian Shorter Catechism, we would accept this as a gospel invitation, but notice the virtue in that definition of saving faith: *"Faith in Jesus Christ is a saving grace, whereby we receive and rest upon him alone for salvation, as he is offered to us in the gospel."* You cannot pass over the blood shed at Calvary and merely receive Christ: "Without shedding of blood is no remission [of sin]" (Hebrews 9:22).

4. Summary.

    a. Be careful, when presenting an invitation, to emphasize the only adequate basis for faith—Calvary.

    b. Never imply that anything other than "coming to our senses" (repentance) about our lostness and having faith in the sufficiency of Christ's sacrifice is necessary for salvation.

    c. Never base assurance on subjective experiences; rather, focus on the promises of God.

    d. Specify that the issue in belief is, "Where is your hope? Upon what are you depending?"

    e. Never neglect the first part of your presentation—the explanation of sin and its consequences—or there will be a temptation to add to the invitation by asking for a "life commitment" to Christ.

ASSIGNMENTS

1. Complete all the assigned memory work. Each of these verses is included for a specific reason. Learn them perfectly, and the references as well.
2. Evaluate a gospel message this week. It may be in church, on television, or on the radio. Was it a clear presentation of the gospel? Did it stress the simple reality of placing our faith in the finished work of Christ? Was the terminology clear?

QUESTIONS FOR DISCUSSION

1. Why is it that you seldom hear the gospel presented without its being adulterated by an additional appeal based on some form of human performance?
2. Right now, discuss with your evangelism partner the role that surrender plays in the life of the Chrisitan.
3. If our appeal is based on "inviting Christ into our lives," what knowledge would the person who attempts this be lacking?
4. What is the difference between being picky about terminology and being convicted about the need for precision? How can one avoid the temptation to get a thrill out of picking apart the witness of others?

PRAYER

Pray that God will burden your heart about precision in presenting the gospel of the grace of God. Thank Him for an objective message that is just as true when we don't feel good as it is when we feel very spiritual.

10

Answering Basic Questions and Objections

Our success does not depend on technique, or on craftiness, or on strong-arm tactics. The gospel *itself* is "the power of God unto salvation to every one that believeth" (Romans 1:16). It needs no embellishment. It is sufficient. It needs only to be clearly presented. Paul majored in this simple, straightforward approach: "Our exhortation was not of deceit, nor of uncleanness, nor in guile: but as we were allowed of God to be put in trust with the gospel, even so we speak; not as pleasing men, but God, which trieth our hearts. For neither at any time used we flattering words, as ye know, nor a cloak of covetousness; God is witness" (1 Thessalonians 2:3-5).

And everywhere Paul preached, people understood. They responded. Saints were added to the church of Jesus Christ. In fact, in this same chapter of Thessalonians we see the predictable response of listeners who are told the good news in a straightforward and objective manner: "For this cause also thank we God without ceasing, because, when ye received the word of God which ye heard of us, ye received it not as the word of men, but as it is in truth, the word of God, which effectually worketh also in you that believe" (1 Thessalonians 2:13).

The gospel works when it is understood and believed. It cannot be believed if it is not understood. Everyone who listens to the gospel brings a different mind set, background, and personality with him. Each has questions that must be resolved. Some have strenuous objections. Take heart. "Fighters" often make the best evangelists after they become Christians! Paul was like that. Once he gave his lifeblood to persecute the church. Then he gave his lifeblood to enlarge the church.

The gospel cannot be believed if it is not understood

129

Don't get off the track

In the basic presentation found in chapters six through eight, there is little mention of how to cope with questions. The rule of thumb is: never get too far off the track. If the question grows out of the subject at hand, answer it. (The quality of your answer ought to be related to the sincerity of the one who inquires.) Unfortunately, anyone who has witnessed frequently knows that some questions are asked merely as smoke screens because the issues are becoming too personal and convicting.

Never allow your basic five-point presentation to become a shouting match or turn into an argument. If someone asks a question and will not accept your answer, ask if you can come back to that question in a little while. Arguments can destroy the continuity and logic of your presentation. But questions must be faced. We believe that the best time to deal with questions is when you ask the final two questions prior to discussing the person's decision to trust Christ as Savior.

Invite questions

You cannot rush ahead of a person's understanding. If he is tuned in, if he is wrestling with the issues of life, take all the time necessary to answer his questions. If you see a look of bewilderment on your listener's face, you ought to amend your question to him so that it sounds something like this: "Mr. Brown, may I ask you a question? Do the things that I have been sharing tonight really make sense to you, or do you have some questions?"

Most questions about the gospel are amazingly similar

Although the questions that people ask are sincere, it is a testimony to human nature to discover how similar most questions are. Almost anyone who has been witnessing for a period of time will agree that questions usually fall into about seven broad categories. We will now list these categories and some possible answers to each issue. Take to heart all of the answers. It is well worth your while to anticipate the questions and have a reasonable answer ready in your mind and heart—indeed, on the tip of your tongue. Be sure that your answer is both logical and biblical.

ONE: THE HEATHEN

"What about the heathen?"

One question commonly asked is *"What about the heathen?"* There are many variations on this theme: "You mean to tell me that those innocent natives in Africa are going to go to hell just because they never heard the gospel?" "Can God condemn those who have never heard?" "God isn't mean. He would never punish anyone!" For this kind of question, we offer the following answers:

1. We must not lose sight of the central issue. The question is not *who may be an exception* to the general rule (that Christ is the only way to heaven). The real issue is *how God says that any man can be saved.* We must start at the beginning by asking the question: How does God save any man? The answer from Scripture: "For I am not ashamed of the Gospel of Christ: for it is the power of God unto salvation to *every one* that believeth" (Romans 1:16).

2. The great argument of Romans 2 is this: God does not hold the heathen accountable for breaking laws that they do not know about. Rather, He holds them accountable only for violating laws that they do know. God can in justice say, "You are inexcusable," because every man has violated his own standards—he does the very things that he points out as abominable in others.

3. When people respond to the light that they have, God sends them more light. This is the magnificent lesson from Acts 10-11. Here we meet Cornelius. He was a Gentile, but he feared God, gave money to the poor, and prayed always (Acts 10:2). He knew something about God, but not enough to be saved. God saw Cornelius respond to the light that he had, so He sent Peter to talk to Cornelius about Christ. God then revealed to Cornelius the fact that Peter would "tell thee words, whereby thou and all thy house shall be saved" (Acts 11:14). Do you see? Cornelius responded to light, but he was not saved until he heard the gospel.

4. Our task is to take the word of Christ, the message of Calvary, to those who have never heard. "You are right to be concerned about the heathen. God is too! He says, 'How then shall they call on him in whom they have not believed? and how shall they believe in him of whom they have not heard? and how shall they hear without a preacher?' (Romans 10:14). Yes, you are right to be concerned about the heathen. Why don't you trust Christ as your Savior and take this message to them?"

5. "I'm not sure about the heathen, but I do know that *you* will never again be able to say, 'No one ever told me!' "

TWO: CHRIST THE ONLY WAY TO GOD

A second common question is *"Is Jesus Christ really the only way to God? That sounds awfully*

The issue: How does God say that any man will be saved?

Cornelius

"Is there only one way?"

131

bigoted." There are variations on this objection, as well: "Everyone will ultimately be saved. . . ." "Hell isn't real; it's just what you make of your life on earth." All these expressions are an attempt to say, "You believe the way you want and I'll believe the way I want and we'll all make it together in the end anyway." To these assumptions we respond:

1. The great questions is: *What is my authority* for believing that anyone will be saved? If it is *my mind*, I can play all the games I want. But there is only one *authoritative source* that tells me about the love of God and about His wonderful heaven. If I accept that source as reliable, I must also believe it when it says: "Neither is there salvation in any other: for there is none other name under heaven given among men, whereby we must be saved" (Acts 4:12).

2. It is not enough to believe something sincerely. The reality of hell does not depend on whether I believe in it any more than does the reality of heaven. Our faith is only as valid as the object of our faith. Faith cannot invent what is real. Faith can only claim the benefits of what is real. We can demonstrate this in two mathematical equations:

The Equation of Sincerity

$$\text{much faith} \quad \times \quad \begin{array}{c} \text{false object} \\ \text{of faith} \end{array} \quad = \quad \text{no reality}$$

$$(1{,}000 \text{ units}) \quad \times \quad (0 \text{ units}) \quad = \quad (0 \text{ units})$$

The Equation of Christianity

$$\text{much faith} \quad \times \quad \begin{array}{c} \text{valid object} \\ \text{of faith} \end{array} \quad = \quad \begin{array}{c} \text{sufficient} \\ \text{faith} \end{array}$$

$$(5 \text{ units}) \quad \times \quad (1{,}000 \text{ units}) \quad = \quad (5{,}000 \text{ units})$$

Sincerity is not enough

No, sincerity is not enough. You have heard of the hunter following deer tracks across the snow in winter. He comes to a frozen river. The ice looks thin. But he *believes* that the ice will support him. Question: When he gets to the middle of the river, will it be his sincerity or the ice that is ultimately the issue? A famous French general is reported to have said, "Facts care little about how they are received by men. Though some embrace them and others reject them, they nevertheless remain facts."

3. It is important to point out that the Bible clearly teaches that if men could be saved in any other way than through faith in the substitution-

ary sacrifice of Jesus Christ, He would have died for no reason. The apostle Paul said, "I do not frustrate [make void] the grace of God: for if righteousness come by the law, then Christ is dead in vain" (Galatians 2:21).

The fact is that Christ did die. God had no morbid desire to see His Son suffer. Yet the Bible teaches that God looked at the horror of the cross with satisfaction (Isaiah 53:11) because it was the ultimate, the sufficient, the only acceptable payment for man's sin. The Bible reveals God's right to determine the ground rules for His mercy and grace (Romans 9:14-20). He has spoken. The issue is: Will men recognize their inability to save themselves and claim instead the perfect provision of Calvary?

4. The same Bible that tells me about the love of Christ tells me about the horrors of hell. The same Bible that teaches me the Golden Rule also insists that "The wrath of God is revealed from heaven against all ungodliness and unrighteousness" (Romans 1:18). I must believe in both or neither.

THREE: PAIN, SUFFERING, AND EVIL

A third common question is *"Why is there so much pain, suffering, and evil in the world?"* People who ask this question wonder whether God is good or whether He is really in control. Sometimes the question is, "Why do the innocent suffer?" or "Why do babies die?" Our answers:

"Why is there suffering?"

1. Men are not robots. God has given to man an authentic moral capacity to choose his destiny. Men have a free will. God is in control, however, because He can use even men's wrong choices for His own ultimate purposes. For example, out of the tragedy of the Second World War emerged the nation of Israel.

2. Evil and suffering in this world have been caused by the wrong choices men have made. God is not the author of suffering; man is. Indeed, the Bible says that offspring as far down the line as the third and fourth generations may be affected by wrong choices and sinful acts. Whenever human beings choose to sin, someone gets hurt; someone suffers.

Evil—the result of wrong choices

3. We must remember that the world is not the way it was when God created it. If it were, we would have to accept one of two conclusions: Either because there is so much evil, God must not be omnipotent (although He may be very

good); or because there is so much evil, God must be sadistic and cruel in His omnipotence. Neither of those conclusions is valid. God created the world—He created man—and said that it was very good. Then man fell into sin and the world became the domain of Satan and selfish, sinful men. The world is not the way God created it. It is presently upside down. It is in rebellion. One day, it will be turned rightside up again.

4. When Christ died on the cross of Calvary, He did so as part of the ultimate solution to the problem of evil. How unfortunate that people blame Christ for the problem of evil when actually He gave His own life to deal a mortal wound to the causes of suffering and evil.

5. You are right to be concerned about the problem of evil, but why not help us win a victory over the forces of evil by following Jesus Christ? God has given us the assurance that one day there will be no more suffering and injustice. In the future, God will wipe away every tear. Pain and sorrow will be forgotten. It will be wonderful. Won't you claim the Lord Jesus Christ as your Savior and join us in the great battle against the powers of darkness and evil?

FOUR: MIRACLES

"Miracles can't happen!"

A fourth common question is *"I don't believe in miracles. How can things happen the way the Bible says they happened? I don't believe that Jonah was swallowed by a fish or that Christ rose from the dead. Let's face it; those things were written at a time when all people were superstitious. That was in a day before scientific enlightenment. Now we know better. I believe in science and in the validity of scientific evidence. Miracles just don't happen!"*

If God is real, we ought to expect miracles

1. Once again, the real question is not, "Do miracles happen?" but, *"Is there a God?"* For if God is real, it is not only *logical* to allow for miracles, *it is foolishness not to expect them.* Is God sovereign over the natural laws He ordained? Has God the right and the power to intervene in the affairs of His creation? The answer: If He is God—yes!

2. There is a dangerous tendency among men to reduce Christianity to a series of moral principles. Christianity is more than that. We are to live in dependence upon God in a moment-by-moment way. The Bible says, "Not that we are sufficient of ourselves to think any thing as of ourselves; but our sufficiency is of God" (2

134

Corinthians 3:5). If God can give me my daily bread today, is it any less of a miracle than those found in Scripture? If miracles cannot happen, then Christ can never change my life—He cannot make me a new creation today. I am doomed to live in enslavement to my own selfishness the rest of my life.

3. Miracles are the only way in which an infinite God could enter into the finite world of man. We call our world the *natural* world—the world of *nature*. God is *supernatural*! Praise God that He is. Everything that we know, we perceive through our natural senses. Miracles are necessary if we are to have any factual or verifiable knowledge of God. As the Lord of nature, our God has chosen to reveal Himself to man by suspending, temporarily, the laws of nature. If He had not revealed Himself through miracles, we could know nothing about Him.

4. Everything that I know about my Lord Jesus Christ, I know because of two great miracles: the revelation of God in the Bible and the incarnation, the revelation of God in human flesh. Apart from these two miracles, I would know absolutely nothing about Jesus Christ.

Everything I know about Christ is a result of two miracles

5. The proof of miracles is not scientific proof but legal proof: the testimony of reliable eyewitnesses. As a pastor, I am often asked to testify in civil court proceedings. They call me a character witness. This is the crux of many legal proceedings. The issue is one person's word against another. In court, if several people who prove to be reliable give the same account of the events in question, the case is won. I cannot say, "I will not believe that Christ rose from the dead unless I can see Uncle Charlie rise from the dead!" Granted, the resurrection of Christ was a unique occurrence. The only way I will become convinced that it happened is to become convinced that the people who were there—who said that they saw the resurrected Christ with their own eyes—were reliable witnesses.

FIVE: ERRORS IN THE BIBLE

A fifth common question is *"Isn't the Bible full of errors?"* Variations on this theme include statements such as "I don't believe the Bible," or "Everybody knows that the Bible contradicts itself," or "It took three hundred years for churchmen to agree on which books should be in the Bible," or "Everyone knows that the Bible is a good book, but it's not necessarily always true."

"The Bible has mistakes, doesn't it?"

135

Stress the Bible's uniqueness

1. When someone asks you if the Bible isn't full of errors, be sure to respond, "Which one in particular did you have in mind?" It is absolutely astonishing that the Bible's critics are the very ones who know the least about Scripture. Almost never will a person be able to recite an assumed contradiction.

2. When someone dares you to prove that the Bible is true, you might respond, "I cannot prove to you that the Bible is true, but I can relate to you why I have found it to be unique; and if you become convinced that the Bible is unique, you will become wonderfully intrigued by what it says. One thing I do know: I have never known it to fail me. Indeed, since I began to read it, I have seen it change my life!"

3. It is possible that there have been mistakes in copying the Scriptures from century to century, but recent archeological discoveries have helped us to determine just how many scribal errors there may be. By comparing the Dead Sea Scrolls with their counterpart books in our Bibles, scholars have come to two conclusions: First, not a single doctrine of Christianity has been affected by mistakes in transcription. Second, all of the differences between the ancient scrolls and their modern counterparts would not fill up even half a page. Yes, for two thousand years God has wonderfully protected His Word.

4. The Bible teaches that it is absolutely *the truth*. Every verse is written for a purpose. Every verse records precisely what God intended to communicate. If there were just a few errors, just a few books that were not really inspired, just a few passages that were purely mythological—would you have confidence in anything the Bible says?

A 95 percent faithful wife!

Would you be satisfied with a wife who is absolutely faithful to you 95 percent of the time? Of course not. Once we allow for errors in Scripture, there is no logical stopping point short of disallowing the entire book.

5. Scripture bears witness to its own validity. "Heaven and earth shall pass away, but my words shall not pass away" (Matthew 24:35). "All scripture is given by inspiration of God" (2 Timothy 3:16). "Holy men of God spake as they were moved [carried along] by the Holy Ghost" (2 Peter 1:21).

6. The key to believing that the Bible is the Word of God is seeing how precisely its prophetic utterances have been fulfilled. *The Bible has never been wrong in its prophecies concerning*

future things. The very world we live in today is a testimony to the accuracy of Bible prophecy. For example, the Bible predicted that the nations of Israel would be scattered, then reborn. Fifty years ago it seemed impossible. Now Israel is a nation. (See Amos 9:14-15).

SIX: THE CHRISTIAN EXPERIENCE IS PSYCHOLOGICAL

A sixth commonly asked question is *"Isn't Christian experience purely psychological?"* The person who asks a question like this may explain what he means by saying that a friend he knows became a Christian because he fell in love with a pretty girl who was a Christian. He may say that every religion brags about miraculous conversions. He may say that strange things happen psychologically to people who get depressed and who then encounter a group of exciting people. He may try to convince you that he once heard a psychologist who said that all hyperreligious people share the same psychological quirks and inadequacies.

1. If I were the only one to have changed the way I have changed, I might be tempted to believe what you are suggesting. But there are Christians who share the same miracle of 'rebirth' who come from every conceivable background and personality type. I have Christian friends who are old, young, optimists, pessimists, outgoing, reserved, emotional, detached, well read, illiterate, rich and poor. There is no way that you can lump them into the same psychological category.

2. One person can be deluded. One person can have a hallucination. But not millions.

3. The crucial issue is: What is the common denominator of these diversified experiences? We suggest that it is faith in the *objective fact* of the historical crucifixion and resurrection of Jesus Christ. It is not psychology that binds Christians together. It is history.

4. Granted, I know people who talk about bizarre things they say have happened to them. It is impossible to argue with a person about his personal experiences. The question that must be raised is: Are his experiences based on historical, objective realities? Are his experiences verifiable to the extent that others who believe the same things have similar experiences?

5. That one person can have a hallucination, no one will deny. But can five hundred people have the same hallucination at the same time?

"It's all psychological!"

The question: Is there a common denominator in Christianity that transcends psychology?

That is the number of people who saw the resurrected Christ in a single encounter.

6. Many people have emotional religious experiences. In fact, it may be said that subjective emotional experiences are common to all religions. But in my years as a pastor, the pattern remains the same. When people base their salvation on the real Christ who died at Calvary, their faith grows long after the emotional experience has ended. On the contrary, when there are no adequate grounds for a man's religious experience, time will always confirm that his faith is worthless. He will give up, admit that he was wrong, and abandon the cause.

SEVEN: A GOOD, MORAL LIFE

"Won't a good life be adequate?"

Finally, a seventh common question is *"Won't a good, moral life get me to heaven?"* When I ask people what they would say if God asked them why He should let them into heaven, I will almost invariably get this answer or a variation on this theme. Some will say, "I live by the Ten Commandments," or "I've always been a dedicated Lutheran," or "I've always tried to do the best I can." Every evangelist needs to have an answer to this matter.

God's standard is perfection

1. God's standard for qualifying for heaven is perfection (Romans 1:18; James 2:10). If I could live an absolutely perfect moral life I could get in by virtue of my works. But no human being can live that way for one single day! I have never lived a perfect day in my life.

2. The Bible confirms our human failure: "There is none righteous, no, not one" (Romans 3:10). If we had to earn our way to heaven by living good (perfect), moral lives, God would be eternally lonely in heaven!

3. In Romans 2, Paul declares that if we kept God's laws perfectly we could qualify for heaven. He then takes twenty verses in Romans 3 to prove that the whole world is guilty before God. *No one qualifies for heaven by keeping the law—by his own good works.* At this point, all of us have the right to sink into despair. Who then can be saved? But Paul then reveals *wonderful news.* In Romans 3:21-22, he declares that *God's righteousness apart from the law is now available to us—if we will believe in what Jesus Christ did for us.* This is the very heart of the Christian message. There are two potential roads to heaven. One is works righteousness: You qualify by being absolutely perfect. (No one can make it to heaven

138

this way.) The second is faith righteousness: You qualify by believing that Jesus Christ paid for your sins when He shed His blood on the cross.

4. The late Dr. Paul Little used to tell a story that beautifully illustrates the folly of trying to get to heaven by living a good, moral life. He likened human attempts to gain glory through moral living to a great swimming contest. Imagine a newspaper announcement that said, "Win a home in heaven by swimming from California to Hawaii!" Now imagine men and women of all shapes and sizes lining up along the West Coast. The gun sounds. The swimmers take to the water. Some can't swim six strokes before they go down. Others are amazingly strong and well conditioned; they swim as far as thirty miles out to sea. *But everyone falls far short of the goal.* Yes, some people do live more uprightly than others, but all fall far short of perfection. "For all have sinned, and come short of the glory of God" (Romans 3:23). Therefore, *faith in Calvary is the only way!* Morality isn't going to get a single soul to paradise.

5. God does expect His own to live a godly life. This life can be lived only by one who is made new—one who has a redeemed life. The only reason that any of us can be good is that Christ lives in us. Do you understand? A righteous life does not cause salvation, it grows out from salvation.

Paul Little's reply

REVIEW OF CHAPTER 10
ANSWERING BASIC QUESTIONS
AND OBJECTIONS

Seven basic questions are repeatedly asked by non-Christians. Variations on these themes make up the bulk of most of the questions you will be asked. Be sure that you have considered each one carefully and can respond to them *logically* and *biblically*.

1. "What about the heathen?" (Variations: "Can God condemn those who have never heard?" "God isn't mean! He would never punish anyone!")
   a. The issue: not who *may be an exception* to the general rule (Christ is the only way), but how God says that a man can be saved. We must start with the method by which God saves a man (Romans 1:16).
   b. God does not hold the heathen responsible for breaking laws that they don't know. Rather, he holds them accountable only for violating laws that they do know (Romans 2).
   c. When people respond to the light they have, God gives them more light (Acts 10-11).
   d. Our task is to take the message of Calvary to those who have never heard (Romans 10).
   e. "I'm not sure about the heathen, but I do know that you will never again be able to say: 'No one ever told me!' "

2. "Is Christ really the only way to God?" (Variations: "Everyone will ultimately be saved." "Hell isn't real; it's just what you make of your life on earth.")
   a. The great question: What is your authority? If it is the Bible, you must accept its teaching that, "neither is there salvation in any other: for there is none other name under heaven given among men, whereby we must be saved" (Acts 4:12).
   b. It is not enough to believe something sincerely. Our faith is only as valid as the object of that faith. (Mention the illustration of the hunter on the ice. It's the *ice* that holds him up — not his faith in it.)
   c. The Bible says that if men could be saved through any other method, then Christ died for no reason (Galatians 2:21).
   d. The same Bible that tells me about the love of Christ tells me about the horrors of hell. I must believe in both or believe in neither.

3. "Why do the innocent suffer?" "Why is there so much pain in the world?"
   a. Men are not robots. God has given them a free moral will.
   b. All evil and suffering in the world have resulted from *man's* making *wrong choices*. It is not God who is the author of suffering, *it is man*.
   c. We must remember that our imperfect world is not the way it was when God created it. God is not responsible for its present misery—sinful men are.
   d. Christ died on the cross as part of the ultimate solution to the problem of evil.

e. "Why not help us win a victory over evil in this world by following Jesus Christ?"

4. "How can miracles be possible?"
   a. The real question: *Is there a God? If God is real,* it is not only *logical* to *allow* for miracles, it is foolishness not to *expect them.*
   b. If miracles can't happen, then Christ can never change my life.
   c. God is *supernatural.* He is the Lord of nature. He has the power to suspend the laws of nature to accomplish His will.
   d. Miracles are the only way in which an infinite Being could enter into the finite world of man.
   e. All that I know about Jesus Christ, I know through two miracles: Scripture and the incarnation.
   f. The proof of miracles is not a scientific experiment, but the testimony of reliable eyewitnesses.

5. "Isn't the Bible full of errors?"
   a. "Which one in particular did you have in mind?"
   b. "I cannot prove to you that the Bible is true, but I can show you why it is unique."
   c. It is possible that there have been mistakes in copying the Scriptures from century to century, but through comparisons of our Bible with the early Dead Sea Scrolls, we find incredibly few copying errors.
   d. The Bible says that it is absolutely *the truth.* If there were a few errors, how would you have any confidence in anything it said?
   e. The key to knowing that the Bible is the inspired Word of God is understanding its prophecy.

6. "Isn't Christian experience only psychological?"
   a. If I were the only one to have changed the way I have, I might wonder about this. But Christians from *every* conceivable background have shared in the same rebirth: old, young, optimistic, pessimistic, outgoing, reserved, college educated, uneducated, rich, poor, and so on.
   b. One person can have a hallucination, but not millions.
   c. The crucial issue is, What is the common denominator for this experience? We suggest that it is faith in the objective fact of the crucifixion and resurrection of Jesus Christ.
   d. My subjective experience is rooted in objective, historical fact.

7. "Won't a good, moral life get me to heaven?"
   a. God's standard for qualifying for heaven is perfection. If I could live a *perfect* moral life, I could get in.
   b. But the Bible says: "There is none righteous, no, not one" (Romans 3:10).
   c. If I can't get to heaven by works righteousness, I must look for another way—the righteousness that is mine by faith (Romans 3:21-22).
   d. Expecting people to get to heaven by living moral lives is like lining up all Americans on the West Coast and expecting them to be able to swim to Hawaii. Some may not swim six strokes, others may swim thirty miles—but *all will fall far short.* Yes, some people live more uprightly than others, but all fall far short of perfection. Therefore, faith in Calvary is the only way.
   e. A good, moral life does not cause salvation, it grows out from salvation.

ASSIGNMENTS

1. Again, as we near the end of our course, review your memory work:
   a. All of your Scripture verses
   b. The three great issues
   c. The five basic truths of the gospel
   d. The questions that enable you to discern a person's spiritual condition
   e. The three issues of the decision itself
2. As you witness this week, be sensitive to the questions and objections people have. You will be amazed how many of the questions fall into the categories covered in this chapter.

QUESTIONS FOR DISCUSSION

1. How do you know when a person's question is merely a smoke screen?
2. Why is it important not to get too far off the track in the middle of your gospel presentation?
3. What broad categories of questions have you been asked that are not covered in this chapter?
4. Are you unsatisfied with the answers offered to any of the questions asked in this chapter? Why?

PRAYER

Thank God for the freedom you have to tell a person that you do not have an answer to his specific question. But thank God also for His Word, which makes most things clear. Ask Him not to let you forget that people are looking for answers. And ask Him to make the love of Christ so evident in your life that people who are searching for answers might be persuaded to ask you for help.

11

Dos and Don'ts in Evangelism

Through the years, I developed fascination for people who come to our front door. Some of them are amusing, others irritating. Strangers at the door can be frightening, disturbing, or winsome. The difference between these responses depends not so much on what is said but on how it is done. If there must be an offensive element in presenting the gospel, let it be the cross and not halitosis! The apostle Paul said it all: "Giving no offence in any thing, that the ministry be not blamed: but in all things approving [commending] ourselves as the ministers of God" (2 Corinthians 6:3-4).

Strangers at the door

In the years of our evangelism workshops at our church, we have made many mistakes. But we are learning. The material in this chapter will highlight the lessons we have learned by experience. Please consider each of these suggestions personally. Your message is important. Let's be genuinely concerned about winning an audience so that the gospel message can have an opportunity to accomplish its life-transforming work.

DOS AND DON'TS IN MEETING AND BECOMING COMFORTABLE WITH A STRANGER

Do believe that this hour represents a life-changing opportunity. Believe God. Pray. Your attitude is contagious. If you don't believe that people will be happy to see you, they probably won't. If you are persuaded that a miracle-working God is going to use your witness to speak to a person's heart, it will affect every aspect of your presentation. Pray while you are still driving toward the prospect's house. Don't wait until you are parked in front.

A life-changing opportunity

143

Your first few minutes

Look sharp!

Crystallize your purpose

Relax!

Don't carry a large Bible when you visit. When an unbeliever sees your large Bible, he is going to be thinking, *What in the world does he intend to do with* that? Rather, slip a New Testament into your pocket or purse. Take it out when you are beginning to present the five central truths of Christianity.

Do believe that everything depends on your first few minutes. People are suspicious of strangers these days. And rightly so. In just a few seconds you must introduce yourself and your purpose in such a way that you are welcome into a home in which strangers are not welcome.

Don't fail to appraise the situation you have just disrupted. These folks have not been waiting for you. Minutes ago they were all doing something else. If a word of apology or transition is in order, feel free to do so. In this way you will be showing courtesy and concern.

Do look sharp—well groomed—confident. Stand in front of a mirror and ask yourself this question: If I were coming to my front door tonight, would I let myself in? Your appearance does make a difference. But in our urban situation, it is just as important not to overdress as it is not to look shabby.

Don't ever ring a doorbell until you have mentally crystallized the purpose for your visit. This is necessary to protect yourself from a momentary memory lapse when the door opens. It is an unbelievable advantage to you if you can announce a reason to be visiting with which your prospect will identify.

Do introduce yourself, your friends, and your church. This communicates that you are not ashamed of what you are doing or who you represent. You are representing one of the fine churches in this person's neighborhood, not a secretive cult.

Don't start your gospel presentation until tensions ease and both parties relax. This, again, is the purpose of looking for points of common interest in the home (furnishings, trophies, hobbies, handmade objects, hints of family activities). When you have convinced your listeners that you are friendly and genuinely interested in their family, they will begin to relax.

Do start at the level of spiritual knowledge the person possesses. For most, this will not be very great. We live in a secular age. Knowledge of the Christian faith is scarce. Take into consideration the age, skills, and mind set of the listener. Don't assume that your listener knows anything about the Bible or about the Lord Jesus Christ.

Don't set a person up. By the time you have asked the questions that reveal a person's spiritual needs, you will understand his hope of heaven. That is the joy of this program. You do not have to bait a person to give you wrong answers. Never ask a person a question like this: "Tell me, Mr. Brown, what do you think you have to do in order to earn your way to heaven?" Do not encourage a person to criticize his former church or his present one. Your success does not depend on vicious attacks at denominations. It depends on the wonder of God's great good news. You will find that some people who have genuine spiritual hunger will tune you out if you slander ideas they once reverenced.

DOS AND DON'TS IN PRESENTING THE GOSPEL

Do make sure that the listener has clarified his hope of heaven before you begin. Before you utter one word of gospel, be sure you have asked the listener to clarify his hope of heaven. When he answers the key question about standing before God, encourage him to repeat his answer. This is important if, after your presentation is over, he tries to convince himself that he has always been a believer. It is my conviction that no genuine, born-again believer will give the wrong answer when questioned about the basis of his hope for eternity.

Don't make your testimony too long. Remember its purpose. You want the listener to be attracted to what you have to say, but it is not the objective of the testimony to tell another all that you know about the Bible.

Do be positive in your approach. How important this is. Yet how rare to find positive Christians! We so easily develop a martyr complex. We so easily persuade ourselves that no intelligent human being with all his proper mental faculties would be interested in Christianity. This is simply not true. Many are looking for answers. When we become unduly defensive about the gospel, we tend to move into one of two extremes. We resort to strong-arm tactics (because we insist that a person needs what he doesn't want), or we make concession after concession (to appeal to the best in the natural man) until the gospel is so watered down that it doesn't save any more.

Your theme is: "I have some good news for

The listener must clarify his hope of heaven before you begin

Be positive in approach!

145

Your listener will detect any tendency to be apologetic

Make it logical

Patiently look for signs of understanding

you!" Never feel ashamed when you are telling someone spiritual truths. You represent a good God. You are talking to a hurting individual. You are the doctor with the right medicine. You must be positive in your approach but absolutely uncompromising in your message. We encourage people to use straightforward words that minimize the possibility of being misunderstood. Don't blush to speak of being saved, the sinfulness of man, hell, the blood of Christ, and the blessed security of the believer.

Don't quote specific references when you are quoting Scripture. Certainly you must always be ready for this response: "Where does it say that?" But your desire in quoting Scripture without references is to free your listener's confused mind as much as is possible so that he can concentrate on what each verse *means.* Simply introduce each verse by saying: "The Bible says . . ." Also, eliminate parts of verses that have no bearing on the issue at hand.

Do make the gospel logical. The five central truths of salvation are logical. One flows from another. Your passion is to hear those beautiful words: "Hey, it all makes sense!" As an aid in emphasizing the logic of your presentation, use your fingers to emphasize truths, and repeat and review often.

Don't move to the next point until you are convinced that the listener understands what you have already said. Yes, it is possible for our presentation to become "canned." When it does, our witness is worthless! What I mean by this is that a person does not lock into spiritual truths just because you once told them to him. Time after time, I will hear something like this: "Pastor Dick, I just can't believe that I sang this great hymn so many years in my old church and never really saw it! Now that I'm saved, it's really precious to me. How could I have missed its message all those years?"

I must emphasize this. Salvation is so much more than a quick recitation of truth and a flippant inquiry about whether you believe it. *So many millions of children are confirmed as responsible members of their churches but are still lost because they have no real understanding of salvation.* I am absolutely persuaded that I can get nine out of ten people to say yes to my religious questions. But I am equally persuaded that if the Holy Spirit is not at work in a person's life and if the issues involved in those questions are not understood, I have absolutely nothing to brag about as I claim another "trophy." Don't talk about Christ until a person understands sin. Don't talk about faith until a person understands substitution. Don't talk about a changed life until a person understands that he is saved by faith alone.

Do illustrate each major truth. We say that this puts meat on the skeleton of the gospel. That's true. We might go even further. Abstract truths can be heard but still remain invisible if they are not brought to life in lively illustrations. It is one thing to talk about sin; it is another to talk about how my children always want their own way. It is one thing to talk about faith; it is another to picture the act of believing as similar to sitting down in a chair in which you have complete confidence. So many times when I am illustrating spiritual truths a person's eyes will brighten as if to say, "Preacher, now I get it!"

Illustrate

Don't be afraid to handle people's questions and objections. On the contrary, welcome them as friends. They are the guarantee that a person is listening. I don't worry about the person who is overly inquisitive. I worry about the individual who is morbidly passive. Don't you lose respect for a person who dodges your questions? I do. There is wonderful peace, however, in having the freedom to admit that you do not have an answer. If you get stumped and the question is valid, why not say: "Say, that's a good question! Do you mind if I do some research on it this week and try to have an answer for you when we get together again?" However, I am convinced that most of the questions that people ask are somehow related to the seven questions covered in the previous chapter. Major on those.

Questions are a sign of interest

There is, however, one vast area of questioning that we have not covered. Often people will ask how Christianity differs from cults or creeds (some of which also claim to be Christian). Without taking a crash course in the doctrines of cults, let me offer this word. All cults and false creeds make their mistake by denying one or more of the following propositions: *First,* the Bible is the *only* Word of God. *Second,* Jesus Christ is the *only* Son of God. And *third,* the blood of Christ is the *only* thing that can pay the penalty for sin. If you remember these cardinal principles of Christianity, you will be able to spot the weaknesses of each of the modern cults immediately.

Answering cultists

Do ask your listener to recite back to you the five truths you have presented to him. Many times

I have been humbled as a pastor. Five hundred people look at me with pleasant smiles on their faces on Sunday morning. Later I ask some of them to tell me what I preached about. What a revelation! Never assume that people who look as if they are listening to you are in fact doing just that. The only way you can know for sure that your listener is indeed listening to you is to ask him to repeat to you the five great truths. You can help him by pointing to each of your five fingers as you have done throughout your presentation.

Don't apologize for the gospel. We have touched on this already. One more word is in order. I have learned that without saying a word I sometimes communicate my attitudes to others. For example, people whom I sincerely love know it. We all communicate on this nonverbal level. That is why you must convince yourself that you have a wonderful message to give to a lost world. Never apologize for this message. It is your proudest possession. Believe that it is the only ultimate hope for the person with whom you are talking.

DOS AND DON'TS IN PRESSING FOR A DECISION

Do believe that salvation involves a decision. Many don't. They cite as evidence Galatians 3:2, which tells us that we are saved simply by "the hearing of faith." We *are* saved that way. Note, however, that we are not saved by "the listening of faith." We can listen to something without hearing a word. My kids do it all the time. When the Bible speaks of hearing, it is talking about choosing to allow into our lives a message to which we are listening.

Whenever we conclude that saving faith involves a choice, we are confronted with the matter of a decision. I am leery of the decision appeals of most evangelists. Their decisions are so often appeals to emotion or appeals to surrender your life to Jesus. Neither of those decisions is acceptable. God asks us to choose to believe that His Son, the Lord Jesus Christ, died on Calvary to pay for our sins in full. That alone must be the decision for which we press.

Don't press for a decision until you are sure that the person understands the gospel. I know that you can never be positively sure that another understands. Yet there are rational, observable indications. The questions he asks, his answers to your questions, his expressions, indeed, his tears, are all clues. Understanding leads to desire. One way you will know that he understands is if the desire to get the matter of salvation settled comes from him, and not from you.

Do be sure that you understand the issues in the decision to be made. I am utterly convinced that the reason so many Christians talk to their friends about Christ but rarely see them saved is that they honestly don't know how to bring into sharp focus the issues in the decision to be made. Again, this decision is not mystical; it is rational. It can be verbalized into three clear propositions: *First,* "Do you take your place before God as a lost, hell-deserving sinner, absolutely powerless to lift a finger to save yourself?" *Second,* "Do you believe that Jesus Christ is the Son of God who died on Calvary to pay the full penalty for your sins?" And *third,* "Do you, right now, claim the free offer of eternal life that God promises to anyone who will place his hope for eternity in the finished work of Christ?"

Be sure you know how to press for a decision

Don't use leading questions. By leading questions we mean those to which no person with an ounce of courtesy could ever reply with a negative answer. All kinds of devices are used to press a person to make a decision. Many are dangerous. Our task is to present the truth and then allow that person to respond to truth that he now understands. If we make it too easy to say yes or impossible to say no, we will violate the very concept of calling men to choose Christ freely.

Don't ask leading questions

Do stress that saving faith involves more than knowledge of facts. Religious people are confused about this. Saving faith demands that knowledge become personalized through choice. We have said it before: "Christ died." That's history. "Christ died for sin." That's theology. "Christ died for *my* sin." That's salvation. Saving faith is the God-given ability to take something that is objectively outside myself and personally claim its benefit. Christ has died for sin. That is fact. God asks me to claim that fact personally and apply it to my own sin problem. It takes an act of choosing to make such a claim.

More than knowledge of facts

Don't allow a seeker to believe that he is saved through prayer. Prayer is beneficial as a tangible way of expressing our faith. But it is faith that saves. In this regard, never ask a person to repeat your prayer, phrase by phrase. Never ask a person to read a printed prayer. We have just said that prayer is beneficial as it outwardly expresses

We are not saved by prayer

inner faith. It must never become a substitute for that inner faith.

Do stress that the issue in salvation is not "Will God accept me?" but "Will I accept His gracious offer?" When people are led to believe that the crux of salvation is "Will God accept me?" they invariably begin to look for ways to make themselves acceptable. This, of course, leads to the pursuit of salvation through performance. After they have tried to change, they throw in the towel and say, "It's no use! It's hopeless! I can never change my life-style enough to be worthy of God's acceptance!"

But God does not ask me to earn His favor. He asks me to believe that His favor is already secured. It is available to all who choose His Son as Savior. How different the issue now becomes. It is no longer that God is turning His back on pleading sinners. It is rather that sinners are turning their backs on a pleading God!

Don't use high pressure tactics if a person is hesitant to make a decision. Here is the excitement of life. We can try to persuade as Paul did, but we cannot force. Each individual has the responsibility to choose his own destiny. Yes, this makes life exciting. It makes witnessing thrilling. We cannot intimidate a person into choosing Christ. We cannot depend on marketing techniques. If we are too forceful, we may cause a person to make an outward decision just to get rid of us. Note: Once a false decision has been made, that person has been inoculated against the possibilities of desiring to make a real decision in the future.

DOS AND DON'TS IN
CONVEYING ASSURANCE

Do show verses on assurance to the one who has made a decision until he has peace. If a decision is real and based on understanding, it is just a matter of enlightenment as the new Christian sees what the Scriptures now guarantee him in the matter of assurance. Scripture speaks for itself here. Become familiar with a half dozen assurance verses, such as John 5:24, John 6:47, Romans 5:1, Romans 8:1, 1 John 5:11-13a, and so forth.

Don't tell a person that he is saved. That is the work of the Holy Spirit. It is a dangerous thing to play God and say: "I guarantee that beyond a shadow of a doubt you are saved!" Such arrogance. You cannot look into another heart. Only

The issue is not: "Will God accept me?"

We cannot force a decision

If one verse fails, use another

Don't tell a person that he is saved

150

God can. When a person sees the issues and is confronted with the right questions (such as: "Now, if you were to die tonight, where would you spend eternity?"), he will tell you that he is saved. There is no greater joy than this. It is absolutely beautiful when a person realizes that he is saved. Saved! Redeemed for all eternity!

Do instruct him that salvation is once for all. One of the greatest perplexities for young believers is this enigma: "If I'm saved, why do I still sin?" Somehow new converts think that they shouldn't sin anymore. What relief to be instructed that there are only two kinds of people in the world: sinners and saved sinners. We won't be perfect until we get to heaven. Thank God that our salvation is not determined by our cessation of sinning. When we believe, we are saved forever; God's Spirit makes His home in our lives forever (John 14:16). We can never lose our salvation. If we did and were to end up in hell, the Holy Spirit would have to go with us to hell, for He abides with us forever. Great verses concerning security are: John 6:39; John 10:28-29; Romans 8:38-39; and Hebrews 10:14.

Salvation is once for all!

Don't allow a person to confuse faith and feelings. This is why the Word of God is so important. It is to be the basis for our assurance—not our feelings. If my assurance were based on my feelings, one day I would think I was saved, the next day I wouldn't. Feelings come and go. Calvary's provision remains the same. The joy of Christianity is the knowledge that when I feel least like I belong to the Lord, I am just as acceptable to Him as I am when I feel preciously near to the heart of God.

Do encourage any new believer to find someone he trusts whom he can tell of his decision. Telling someone else what has happened on the very first day of his Christian life is a vital part of the new convert's getting off to a good start in this great new adventure. It is positively liberating to tell someone for the first time that you are saved, a new creature in Christ, and on your way to heaven. It is perfectly fine to tell a friend who already is a Christian about your new life. But do it today.

Tell someone today

Don't skim over the issue of assurance. If a person is willing to claim Christ as Savior, he is entitled to assurance immediately. But some people are so saturated with religion that they can hardly bring themselves to say, "I'm saved!" However, it is important that they gain this assur-

Salvation is not perfection

ance as soon as possible, because assurance is the test of genuine faith.

Do assure a new convert that salvation is not perfection. We have already covered this topic in detail. Just one more word. One of the first things that a new believer ought to be taught is what causes sin in the believer's life and how to deal with this impulse. It is liberating to see that no Christian has to be the slave of sin. "Sin shall not have dominion over you" (Romans 6:14).

DOS AND DON'TS IN THE MATTER OF FOLLOW-UP

Make your exit sweet

Do make your exit sweet, whether or not a person trusts Christ as Savior. If a person is cold, thank him for the privilege of his time. If he shows signs of curiosity, be sure to inquire about the possibility of coming back for another visit. If a person has trusted Christ, *you have no choice but to return and follow up on this new life.* This is the time of greatest need. This is the time of satanic assault. This is the time of confusion and perplexity. Ironically, this is precisely the time at which most churches fail.

Don't walk away from a person who has just received Christ as Savior. If you care enough to reach him, you must care enough to teach him. You may find that another Christian you know has a personality that is similar to your new convert's. But you must take the responsibility of bringing them together. Now that you have a newborn child, your task is not over—it is just beginning.

Be conservative

Do be conservative in your estimation of what has taken place that evening. Great damage is done when a loved one who has been on everyone's prayer list for years finally makes a decision and the one who has led him to Christ tells the whole world: "Jim's whole life has changed!" First of all, time always tells the story. If a decision is real, it will stand the test of time. Second, change often comes slowly to a new believer. If he believes that five hundred people are watching him, he will feel great pressure (and find himself chafing against a church's legalistic expectations of him).

Do have concrete suggestions for a new believer. There are basics of the Christian life about which we all need to know. Every Christian needs to learn the importance of Bible study, prayer, and fellowship. Be sure that you offer a new believer a Bible if he doesn't have one. Suggest that

152

he begin his new life by reading a chapter of the gospel of John each day. Ask him if you can get together again soon to discuss his questions on the gospel of John. Invite him out to church un-apologetically. And, by all means, leave your phone number with him.

REVIEW OF CHAPTER 11
DOS AND DON'TS IN EVANGELISM

Dos

1. In meeting a person
   a. Do believe that this hour represents a life-changing opportunity. Believe God. Pray.
   b. Do believe that everything depends on your first few minutes.
   c. Do look sharp—well groomed—confident.
   d. Do introduce yourself, your friends, and your church.
   e. Do start at the level of spiritual knowledge the person possesses.
2. In presenting the gospel
   a. Do make sure that the listener has clarified his hope of heaven before you begin.
   b. Do be positive in your approach.
   c. Do make the gospel logical.
   d. Do illustrate each major truth.
   e. Do ask your listener to recite back to you the five truths you have told him.
3. In pressing for a decision
   a. Do believe that salvation involves a decision.
   b. Do be sure that you understand the issues in the decision to be made.
   c. Do stress that saving faith involves more than knowledge of facts.
   d. Do stress that the issue in salvation is not "Will God accept me?" but "Will I accept God's gracious offer?"
4. In conveying assurance
   a. Do show verses on assurance to the one who has made a decision until he has peace.
   b. Do instruct him that salvation is once for all.
   c. Do encourage any new believer to find someone he trusts whom he can tell about his decision.
   d. Do assure a new convert that salvation is not perfection.
5. In following up
   a. Do make your exit sweet, whether or not a person trusts Christ as Savior.
   b. Do be conservative in your estimation of what has taken place that evening.
   c. Do have concrete suggestions for a new believer.

Don'ts

1. In meeting a person
   a. Don't carry a large Bible when you visit.
   b. Don't fail to appraise the situation you have just disrupted.
   c. Don't ever ring a doorbell until you have mentally crystallized the purpose of your visit.
   d. Don't start your gospel presentation until tensions ease and both parties relax.
   e. Don't set a person up.
2. In presenting the gospel
   a. Don't make your testimony too long.
   b. Don't quote specific references when you are quoting Scripture.

c. Don't move to the next point until you are convinced that the listener understands what you have already said.

d. Don't be afraid to handle people's questions and objections.

e. Don't apologize for the gospel.

3. In pressing for a decision

a. Don't press for a decision until you are sure that the person understands the gospel.

b. Don't use leading questions.

c. Don't allow a seeker to believe that he is saved through prayer.

d. Don't use high-pressure tactics if the person is hesitant to make a decision.

4. In conveying assurance

a. Don't tell a person that he is saved. That is the work of the Holy Spirit.

b. Don't allow a person to confuse faith with feelings.

c. Don't skim over the issue of assurance.

5. In following up

a. Don't walk away from a person who has just received Christ as Savior.

ASSIGNMENT

Write up your own list of dos and don'ts in evangelism.

PRAYER

Pray that Christ may be seen in you. Ask God to make Christ known through what you say. Ask also for the grace to be able to know the difference between the offense of the gospel and being offensive. Pray that God will help you to take little things seriously and that God will help you to care enough about souls to represent the great Lover of our souls faithfully.

12

Personal Follow-up— A Challenge for an Individual

The importance of a follow-up plan

You care. That's why you are interested in evangelism. That's why you are studying this manual. But caring people can still be unproductive. This happens when concern fails to be focused and channeled. It is one thing to care. It is another to have a plan.

There is much talk today about follow-up. The subject of man-to-man discipleship has been popular since the days when Dawson Trotman began his fruitful Navigator ministry. He had a plan.

It is impossible for us to develop a plan effectively without crystallizing our goals. That's where we begin. You have just seen a soul trust Christ. Fantastic! There is no experience like it. You suddenly realize that this makes you a *parent*! As such, you see that your responsibility for this new life is not over—it has only just begun. It's time to develop a master plan that will lead this new believer into progressive maturity. Your plan must be based on concrete goals. Consider these seven basic goals of personal follow-up:

Seven goals of follow-up

1. Reinforcing the convert's understanding of the basis for complete assurance of salvation
2. Acquainting the convert with a gospel-preaching church and seeing him participate in it
3. Seeing the convert establish Christian friendships and relationships
4. Seeing the convert participate in a small-group Bible study
5. Helping the convert understand the basic principles of the Christian life

156

6. Seeing the convert learn to make exciting discoveries in personal Bible study
7. Answering the convert's questions

Before we can begin to implement these goals we must have access to a life. That's where follow-up begins. As soon as a person accepts Christ as Savior, the one who has led him to Christ must be straightforward in his approach to follow-up. He must clarify the need for continuing to meet together. "Bill, I rejoice in your decision to trust Christ as Savior. The Bible says that when a person becomes a Christian, he becomes, as it were, a spiritual baby. Now he needs to grow. He needs food, knowledge, training, love, and encouragement. I would feel privileged to be able to meet with you for a time in order to help you get started in the great adventure that we call living the Christian life. Is it OK with you if we meet together on a regular basis?"

When both parties have been able to agree on a time (weekly or biweekly) you can begin to achieve your goals.

Access to a life

REINFORCING THE CONVERT'S UNDERSTANDING OF THE BASIS FOR COMPLETE ASSURANCE OF SALVATION

1. The basis of assurance

This, of course, is the most basic issue you face. If you fail here, you fail in everything. There are four important lessons a new Christian must learn in order to be able to delight in the blessedness of assurance.

LESSON ONE

First, *he must learn that salvation does not have its base either in personal feelings or in personal performance. (Study each Scripture reference with your disciple.)*

The object of our faith is *what God says* ("the record," 1 John 5:10) about *what Christ did* (1 John 4:10).

God is *no respector of persons* (Romans 2:11). He will save all who claim His promise for themselves (Romans 10:13). He promises that He will save all who make their only hope of eternal life Christ's finished work at Calvary.

When I believe (claim Christ's blood as payment for my sin by personal choice), God makes two great judicial reckonings: He declares me to be *forgiven*—the *removal* of a *negative* (Acts 13:38-39), and He imputes to me Christ's

What God says about what Christ did

157

righteousness—the *bestowal* of a *positive* (2 Corinthians 5:21).

Thus, I am saved by *decree,* not by *degree!* God declares me to be righteous (Romans 3:24; "justified" means "declared righteous").

When I reckon these things to be true with my mind, it will undoubtedly result in joy and peace. First comes the fact—then the emotional response.

LESSON TWO

Second, *when a person is saved he is secure in that salvation forever.*

Nothing can separate me from Christ's love (Romans 8:35-39).

Nothing can take me from Christ's hand (John 10:27-29).

Christ said: "of all which he [the Father] hath given me I should lose nothing" (John 6:39).

Christ gave us His Holy Spirit, who (He promises) will abide in us forever (John 14:16).

God saw the end of our salvation even before we believed. All "whom he did foreknow, he also did predestinate to be conformed to the image of his Son" (Romans 8:29).

We are sealed by the Holy Spirit until the day of redemption (Ephesians 1:13-14).

We are kept by the power of God (1 Peter 1:5).

A place in heaven is reserved for us (1 Peter 1:4).

LESSON THREE

Third, *we must teach new believers the nature of positional truth.* Many things are true about us as Christians simply because God sees us as united to His Son. We cannot *feel* these things to be true. They can become of practical benefit to us only as we *reckon* (or *count*) them to be so.

We are "blessed . . . with all spiritual blessings in heavenly places in Christ" (Ephesians 1:3).

God has given us *all things* that pertain to life and godliness (2 Peter 1:3-4), but we are to *add* to them (2 Peter 1:5-8). Peter is simply saying that we are to put into practice in our daily lives things that God has said are true about us already. These things are of no value to us unless we claim them to be true and begin putting them to work.

Thus, we are to see ourselves as dead to sin (Romans 6:6); then we are to put this knowledge to work practically—reckon it to be true (Romans 6:11).

Saved by decree, not by degree

Nothing can separate from Christ's love

Positional truth

158

Fourth, *we must teach new believers the cause of their defeats, their sins, their discouragements.*

Every Christian has three powerful enemies: the world (1 John 2:15-16), the flesh (Galatians 5:16), and the devil (1 Peter 5:8-9).

The *world* does not refer to the physical universe; rather, it refers to all that keeps a man from seeking the things of God. It is the value system of sinful men.

The *flesh* is the impulse to sin which lives in every believer (see Romans 7:15-17). Note: The impulse itself is not sin. Praise the Lord, we can control and master the impulse.

The *devil* is a real, personal adversary. He pretends to offer us pleasure, but he has only one purpose in mind—our total destruction (1 Peter 5:8).

Christians can and do sin. Their sin can lead to guilt and discouragement. God's solution is to confess our sins—deal with them—take them back to Calvary (1 John 1:9). But no sin in a believer's life will ever result in loss of his salvation. We must also teach new believers that part of their discouragement is due to the subtle attacks of the enemy. Teach them the lessons of Ephesians 6:10-17.

ACQUAINTING THE CONVERT WITH A GOSPEL-PREACHING CHURCH AND SEEING HIM PARTICIPATE IN IT

2. The importance of the right church

Your new acquaintance will probably have a religious background. If he is under thirty, he will most likely have rejected that background. It is *imperative* that you talk with him about the difference between religion and Christianity. To him religion means rules, boredom, liturgy, and financial appeals. You want him to know that Christianity involves fellowship, worship, knowledge, and most important, a whole life. Christianity is not a weekly activity. It is a new way of looking at everything—job, purpose, future, family, friends, success, and so forth.

It is almost impossible for the new believer to understand this way of life until he becomes familiar with a fellowship of believers. Never apologize for your church. It is a community of the most precious people in the world. It is accomplishing the most important task in the world.

A church: the best way to communicate that Christianity is a total way of life

Jay Adams has rightly observed that a robber ceases to be a robber only when his "livelihood" is replaced with a productive means of earning a

159

Most people who reject church have never attended one like yours!

living. I think that we expect the impossible when we try to teach Christianity to people without urging them to see it in action in a local church. Like the robber, the new believer will change as he is given the opportunity to fill his life with exciting activities and new challenges.

Most people have never seen a church like yours and ours. Perhaps they are startled by our friendliness, our informality, the centrality of Bible teaching, the abundance of activities. Yes, some are bothered by how noisy we may be. But they cannot deny that they see happy people, motivated people—people who are enjoying a whole new way of life.

The matter of a church is a sticky issue to some people. This is especially true of older folks who have established comfortable patterns and are solidly locked into traditions. But here are a few insights in encouraging a new believer to become a participant in a Bible-believing church:

1. Discover his present pattern of church attendance.

2. Ask him to describe his feelings about his church.

3. Explain the difference between religion and Christianity.

4. Relate how your church is made up of people who became discouraged with religion and looked for a vital Christian community of true believers.

5. Invite your friend to your church service— and then to dinner.

6. Be sure to offer to pick him up. If he drives, arrange for a place to meet him before the service.

7. Do not introduce him to hundreds of people, but select a few friends whom you feel he will enjoy.

8. Do not invite him to both church and Sunday school the first week.

9. Be sure to notify the pastor that you are bringing a friend. Introduce your pastor to him.

10. Don't belittle a single aspect of your worship service. Yet, be free to express that your entire fellowship is working hard to improve some areas.

11. Invite him to attend one of your church's informal activities.

12. Be willing to sit with him in the services for as long as you feel that this is important to him.

13. If he has a commitment to a liberal church

for the present, be sure to invite him to your Sunday evening services.

14. Finally, do not invite him to any church that you cannot enjoy. If *you* are interested in evangelism, find a church that you can be proud to recommend to those you lead to the Savior.

SEEING THE CONVERT ESTABLISH CHRISTIAN FRIENDSHIPS AND RELATIONSHIPS

Sometimes I am called a matchmaker. That designation is not all bad. It is a wonderful joy to see two people meet, fall in love, marry. It's a delight to see relationships of all kinds develop within the context of a church. Every other month we have a Mix and Match Fellowship. The purpose is to ask young people to invite those over forty to their homes and to urge our older people to invite the young adults to theirs. It's a special kind of evening.

Christians are a distinct minority in our society. Christians need each other. Blessed is the church that can meet the friendship needs of the lonely people who visit there. This is a creative process.

My wife and I often plan to have couples over who may be a particular blessing to some new people. You have a similar responsibility. You are the matchmaker. Your life will take on a whole new sense of excitement as you try to guide your disciple into new, solid, Christian friendships. Invite some people over for dinner to meet him. As you organize your guest list, take into account such things as marital status, children, neighborhood, vocation, educational background, personality type, economic situation, and so forth. Why? Because fellowship means commonness. The more people have in common, the more likely it is that friendship can take root.

SEEING THE CONVERT PARTICIPATE IN A SMALL-GROUP BIBLE STUDY

Several years ago, when we first came to our church, we had a few young people. In the course of that first year we grew from a Sunday school class of twelve to one of sixty. The next year the class jumped to over one hundred. Many have come, many have gone. There are stories of happy successes, and there are some stories of soul-rending disappointments. But a handful of folks who began to attend our church in those days are now our leaders. They are dynamos for Christ. One of them recently remarked to me,

"Pastor, I'm convinced that the reason some of us have grown so rapidly and developed such deep friendships is that we were part of a small home Bible study each Friday night. The study meant so much to me as a new believer!"

The church had better wake up to reality. Historically, when the church fails to meet a need, a parachurch group rises up to meet the need. That is the story of the Navigators, high school Bible clubs, women's organizations, and so forth. Now from coast to coast the living-room Bible study concept has erupted. When these studies become substitutes for churches, they are dangerous. But when they are sponsored by churches and become vital arms of churches, they can become a marvelous help in follow-up. Many churches have divided their entire adult fellowship into small Bible-study groups. The blessing is obvious. Those churches are growing.

You have led a soul to Christ. You want to see him grow. Pray him right into a small-group Bible study. You may want to follow these suggestions:

1. Ask your pastor to publish a list of all the studies conducted by local church members in the course of a week. The list ought to include day, time, place, name of host and hostess, name of teacher, topics studied, and any additional comments that would be helpful, such as, "We study out of the Roman Catholic version of the Bible."

2. Ask your newborn friend to tell you what he believes to be his basic spiritual needs at this time. Explain to him how a small-group Bible study could be used of God to meet those needs.

3. Explain to him why some Christians you know have grown so quickly. Others stay the same year after year. A small study forces each participant to interact with the Scriptures.

4. Introduce your friend to the teacher of the class when you see him on Sunday.

5. Be willing to attend a class session or two if it is possible to fit it into your schedule.

HELPING THE CONVERT UNDERSTAND THE BASIC PRINCIPLES OF THE CHRISTIAN LIFE

"If any man be in Christ, he is a new creature: old things are passed away; behold, all things are become new" (2 Corinthians 5:17). As Dr. Dave Breese says so articulately: "It is one thing to *be* a Christian, it is quite another to *think* like a Christian." Many who are truly saved never do make

A new believer cannot get to know hundreds, but he can feel comfortable with a handful

5. Learning basic principles

this transition. They remain bound to tradition, earthly philosophies, and pragmatic logic.

But James tells us that there is a "wisdom that is from above" (James 3:17). Paul's constant supplication for his readers is that the *eyes of their understanding might be enlightened* (Ephesians 1:18). The greatest joy of the Christian life is making progressive discoveries about reality from God's standpoint. We soon learn that things are not as they appear. We are to walk by faith, not by sight.

At this point it might be helpful to list some books that reveal some of the wonderful ways of God to us. Certainly they are no substitute for Scripture, but you ought to be familiar with them so that you can recommend them to new Christians:

Born to Grow, by Larry Richards. Wheaton, Ill.: Victor, 1974.

Design for Discipleship series, by The Navigators. 6 booklets. Colorado Springs, Colo.: Navpress, 1973.

Discover Your Destiny, by Dave Breese. 1965. Reprint. Chicago: Moody, 1972.

First Steps in the Christian Faith, by the staff of the Correspondence School, Moody Bible Institute. 12 lessons. Chicago: Moody Bible Institute, [1957].

Grace and Truth, by W. P. Mackay. Abridged ed. Chicago: Moody, n.d. (Available in quantity from Pacific Garden Mission, 646 South State Street, Chicago, Illinois 60605.)

Now That I Believe, by Robert A. Cook. Chicago: Moody, 1956.

Salvation from Start to Finish, by James M. Gray. Chicago: Moody, n.d.

A Survey of Bible Doctrine, by Charles Caldwell Ryrie. Chicago: Moody, 1972.

What Christians Believe, by staff members of the Emmaus Bible School. Chicago: Moody, 1949.

Gary W. Kuhne's *Dynamics of Personal Follow-up* (Grand Rapids: Zondervan, 1976) can help you master personal follow-up procedures.

SEEING THE CONVERT LEARN TO MAKE EXCITING DISCOVERIES IN PERSONAL BIBLE STUDY

If an individual is going to gain maximum benefit from Bible study, he must understand what God wants to accomplish through the Word in his life every day. From God's point of view, the Bible meets four personal needs daily.

These books are helpful tools for young Christians

6. Personal Bible study

**The Bible meets
four basic needs:
1. Communication
2. Nourishment
3. Insight
4. Protection**

Expect opposition

**The key to
personal Bible
study—making
discoveries**

1. *Communication*—the Bible is the key to *fellowship* with God (1 John 1:3).

2. *Nourishment*—the Bible is the key to *spiritual growth* (1 Peter 2:2).

3. *Insight*—the Bible is the key to *wisdom and understanding* (1 Corinthians 2:14).

4. *Protection*—the Bible is the key to *spiritual strength* (in the daily battle against Satan) (Ephesians 6:17).

With those objectives in mind, consider these suggestions for a meaningful devotional life:

1. Expect opposition. Somehow, unless you approach this matter of Bible study with real resolve, it will "mysteriously" be neglected and pushed out of the way. Satan fights.

2. New believers ought to be advised to use a modern translation or paraphrase of the Bible as a companion volume to a more word-for-word translation. We must confess that learning the language of the King James Version is often more difficult than we are willing to admit. However, a paraphrase must never become a substitute for a word-for-word translation.

3. Analyze this question: What brings excitement in Bible study? The answer is always the same—*discovery*. It doesn't matter how long I read; what matters is that I discover something vital.

4. Discoveries were meant to be told to others. Find a Bible-study partner (or a small group of friends) with whom you can meet regularly for the purpose of telling each other your discoveries.

5. Never open your Bible without clarifying your purpose. Are you looking for a solution to a doctrinal tension? For encouragement? For guidance? For knowledge? For the key that unlocks a book or chapter in the Bible?

6. Never read your Bible without a pen in hand. If you do not want to mark up your Bible, have paper handy. Record or underline such things as the sequence of events, repetition of words, ideas, verses, key verbs, commands, exhortations, and so forth.

7. Remember, no Bible-study methods can aid a cold heart. There are things you can do to prepare your heart. One thing you can do is pray. Begin your study by communing with God. Another thing you can do is study in a quiet place without distraction—never with the TV on. Also, have your devotions early in the day, when your mind is alert. In addition, develop your ability to concentrate on one thing at a time. And finally, be

sure that the lighting is good, that there are no flies in the room, and that the temperature is right.

8. Purchase some basic tools for effective Bible study. You've got an open Bible, a piece of paper, a pen in hand. But that's just the beginning. Here are the basic tools that I use to enhance my personal devotions:

A Bible dictionary: For the novice, *Unger's Bible Dictionary,* 3rd edition, by Merrill F. Unger (Chicago: Moody, 1966), or the *New Bible Dictionary,* edited by J. D. Douglas (Grand Rapids: Eerdmans, 1962), will suffice. For the more advanced, the *International Standard Bible Encyclopedia,* revised edition, 5 volumes, edited by James Orr (Grand Rapids: Eerdmans, 1930), is a must. The purpose of a Bible dictionary is to shed light on any word, topic, or issue related to the Bible.

Expository Dictionary of New Testament Words, by William E. Vine (Old Tappan, N.J.: Revell, n.d.): What makes this tool so valuable is that you don't need to know Greek to use it. Simply look up the English word (from the King James Version) and this work will tell you the Greek words used, their etymologies, and where in Scripture they are used.

A good concordance: Get *Young's Analytical Concordance to the Bible,* revised edition, by Robert Young (Grand Rapids: Eerdmans, 1955), *Strong's Exhaustive Concordance of the Bible,* by James Strong (Nashville: Abingdon, n.d.; New York: Nelson, 1977), *Englishman's Greek Concordance of the New Testament* (Grand Rapids: Zondervan, n.d.), *Englishman's Hebrew and Chaldee Concordance of the Old Testament* (Grand Rapids: Zondervan, n.d.). Use of these concordances will help you find every location in the Bible where a certain word is found.

New Testament Survey, revised edition, by Merrill C. Tenney (Grand Rapids: Eerdmans, 1961): Valuable as a help for understanding when and why each New Testament book was written.

Old Testament Times, by Roland K. Harrison (Grand Rapids: Eerdmans, 1970), or *The Old Testament Speaks: Old Testament History and Literature,* by Samuel J. Schultz (New York: Harper & Row, 1970): The two counterparts of Tenney's *New Testament Survey.*

Charles R. Erdman's devotional commentaries on each New Testament book (Philadelphia: Westminster, 1916-36):

165

7. Encourage questions

ANSWERING THE CONVERT'S QUESTIONS

Much of our conversations with a new Christian tends to be one-sided. We talk and he listens. Develop the ability to become interested in another life. His questions are important. You want to know the things that are on his heart. One way to do this is to urge him to write down questions that come to his mind during the week. Then go over those questions, together. You will *both* learn.

THE MECHANICS OF FOLLOW-UP

The time for follow-up

The time. A person's sex, age, and occupation will be determining factors in when you can get together. During the course of the last eight years of my ministry, I have met for breakfast with a young man or two almost every day. I have found that this is the best time for most men. They work during the day. They have families to enjoy in the evenings. During these years I have met with hundreds of men. I am richer because of it. We talk, we read, we pray.

Ladies usually have a flexible schedule, although this is changing. I recommend lunchtime or early afternoon. When married couples are involved (and the couple *ought* to be involved every time, even when only *one* of them is saved), there is practically no way to meet other than during an evening.

The place to meet

The place. I visit a restaurant close to our church so frequently that we refer to it as The Annex. People are at ease in a public place. It is comfortable to talk when each of you is holding a cup of coffee. I offer a word of caution. If you meet for one-on-one discipleship in a restaurant, be sure to select one that plays only easy-listening music. It is difficult to concentrate when loud, popular music is blaring.

It is wonderful if you can meet in a house. But do not meet in a house where it is impossible to secure privacy. Nor should you meet in a location in which you are certain to meet hostility. You must both be free to talk about the tender and deep things of the heart.

Transforming a convert into a friend

The procedure. Remember, you are transforming a *convert* into a *friend.* This requires hours of two-way, casual conversation. Take plenty of time for this. Then open your Bibles for study for fifteen to twenty minutes. Close with a word of prayer.

166

The subject matter. Proceed along two lines simultaneously. First, tell your friend to write down all the questions that perplex him about his new life. You will be surprised how many questions come up. Most new believers wonder why their families are not more excited about these things. Others want to discuss the misconceptions they have about the Christian life. Still others will ask a flood of chapter-and-verse questions. Always be ready to admit that you don't have an answer but are willing to search for it.

Second, proceed along a more systematic line. We suggest three kinds of topics. First, you might want to *study a book of the Bible*—John, for example. Second, you might want to study *a different doctrine of Christianity each week,* following, for example, a book such as *What Christians Believe.* Finally, you may want to deal with *a practical issue* each week—for example, "Is a Christian supposed to feel saved?" Make your selection on the basis of the preference of your disciple. Then, be sure to become thoroughly familiar with your material in advance.

SUMMARY: FOUR QUESTIONS THAT DETERMINE THE SUCCESS OF FOLLOW-UP

Many books have been written on the techniques of follow-up. It is a wonderful subject; but like so many other subjects of current interest, I think it suffers from a rather acute case of theological elephantiasis. When all is said and done, the key to follow-up is not *special knowledge,* it is *special concern.* I confess, frankly, that those in our congregation who, like Apollos of old, "helped them much which had believed" (Acts 18:27) have never read a book on follow-up. They have fused common sense with the love of Christ. They recognize that newborn believers are in a precarious position. They have no Christian friends, little knowledge of the Scriptures, no grounding in an evangelical tradition, and plenty of people who will discourage them from walking with Christ in every way that they can. Common sense dictates that a new believer needs the reinforcement of the Christian community—especially one member of it: you.

Therefore, let's be practical. Do you really want to know how to evaluate your follow-up efforts? Prayerfully ask yourself these questions:

1. *First, have you made a friend out of a convert?* It is one thing to thank God for a soul, it is

1. Have you made a friend?

2. Can he talk freely about his conversion?

another thing to thank God for a friend. Most of the new converts at our church endured those early months through the encouragement, love, and prayers of a Christian friend. Don't make a fatal mistake and think that because a new believer is indwelt by the Holy Spirit he will have an easy time adapting to the Christian life. Time after time I am confronted in my office by someone who trusted Christ several years ago but is nowhere today because he simply was not cared for by those responsible for his salvation. This is inexcusable.

But it is understandable. People haven't changed. We name our sons after *Paul* and our dogs after *Apollos*. Paul was the evangelist. All Apollos did was help Christians to grow! Where would some of us have been without an Apollos to help us? Look at 1 Corinthians 3:6: Paul says, "I have planted, Apollos watered; but God gave the increase." The picture is a field. The seed is planted. It breaks through the soil, rich and green. But then drought comes. There is no water; there is no waterer. Green turns to brown, growth stops, leaves begin to shrivel up. But then . . . water! The crop is saved. *May God give the church millions of Apolloses.*

2. Second, is your new Christian friend able to see and talk about the centrality of his conversion? Many people limp into the Christian life and live like pagans for years simply because no one told them that Calvary puts an end to the old and signals the beginning of the new. Again it must be said: Don't be ashamed of a single aspect of Christianity. Christ is altogether lovely. We look forward to a blessed hope! On the other hand, it is the old sin life that kills, alienates, robs us of joy and purpose.

You must talk in the frankest possible terms about being *saved*. Show every new Christian glorious passages like these: "Shall we continue in sin, that grace may abound? God forbid. How shall we, that are dead to sin, live any longer therein?" (Romans 6:1-2). "Knowing this, that our old man is crucified with him, that the body of sin might be destroyed, that henceforth we should not serve sin" (Romans 6:6). "Therefore if any man be in Christ, he is a new creature: old things are passed away; behold, all things are become new" (2 Corinthians 5:17). "And you hath he quickened [made alive], who were dead in trespasses and sins" (Ephesians 2:1). "Giving thanks unto the Father, which hath made us meet

168

[fit] to be partakers of the inheritance of the saints in light: who hath delivered us from the power of darkness, and hath translated us into the kingdom of his dear Son" (Colossians 1:12-13).

The more a new believer is able to see the centrality of conversion, the more quickly he will grow. Once he was dead. Now he is alive. Once lost, now found. Once a slave, now a son. Encourage him to talk about being saved. He must be urged to tell others about this fabulous miracle as soon as possible. Let him begin by telling Christians about his conversion. Next he can communicate this message to his loved ones. Finally, the world is his audience. Never feel that your follow-up has been successful until your convert can freely talk about his Christianity.

3. *Third, is the convert growing in his appreciation of the Bible?* Christians cannot live without food. The Bible is our bread. The key to Bible study is *discovery*. When your devotions are exciting it is because you are making discoveries. When they are dull it is because your discoveries have ceased.

A person has to be trained to make discoveries for himself. Part of that training is simply listening to the discoveries of a spiritual Christian. You have won a victory when a new Christian begins to think, *How did he find all of that in those few verses? Wow! That's for me! This book is loaded! I'm going to search out its treasures for the rest of my life!*

But you can help by teaching a person how to look for discoveries. Challenge him to find certain key things in the portion of Scripture he will be reading next week. For example, we start new Christians in the gospel of John. If you adopt this approach, these are some of the questions to which a new believer can discover answers:

John 1: How is Christ described in the first fourteen verses?
What two conclusions did John the Baptist arrive at concerning Jesus Christ?
What discoveries about Christ were made by Andrew, Peter, Philip, and Nathaniel? What did they do with their discoveries?

John 2: What is so special about Christ's first miracle?
What did Jesus mean when He said: "Destroy this temple, and in three days I will raise it up" (v. 19)?

3. Does he love his Bible?

169

4. Is he linked to a body of believers?

It's a two-way street!

John 3: How did Jesus tell Nicodemus that a man can be born again?

As you help a person to focus his energy and guide him into the thrill of finding these truths for himself, you will be helping your friend toward making a giant step in his appreciation of the Scriptures.

4. *And fourth, does your newly saved friend feel comfortable in the fellowship of the body of believers?* You may think this is a minor issue. I don't. Time after time I have seen what happens to an established believer when he begins a new job that forces him to work on Sundays. The results are always devastating. Enjoying the corporate worship experience of a local body of believers (rather than listening to a gospel broadcast on TV) is basic to growth. No matter what the reason—sickness, travel, depression, job—when a person is denied the experience of corporate worship and fellowship, his spiritual life suffers.

If this is true of established believers, you can begin to understand the vital role of the local church in the life of a new believer. Never feel that your church has a corner on the market of truth. Never let a new convert think so either. Your church is just one of thousands that are faithfully serving Christ.

Do not make the issue your church. What is important is that your friend become a part of a vital fellowship of believers somewhere. Be sure that your heart is pure. Do not tolerate an ulterior motive. You are seeking his good and Christ's glory, not the personal praise of your church friends.

I close with this reminder about one-on-one follow-up. You will miss the world's biggest blessing if you think that your role in this process is exclusively to be the teacher. Ask the Lord to teach you precious lessons about Himself from every meeting you have with a new believer. You will find that you will be receiving more than you give.

REVIEW OF CHAPTER 12
PERSONAL FOLLOW-UP—
A CHALLENGE FOR AN INDIVIDUAL

1. You care. But along with concern must come a plan. And your plan must be based on concrete goals. There are at least *seven basic goals* of personal follow-up:
   a. Reinforcing the convert's understanding of the basis for complete assurance of salvation
   b. Acquainting the convert with a gospel-preaching church and seeing him participate in it
   c. Seeing the convert establish Christian friendships and relationships
   d. Seeing the convert participate in a small-group Bible study
   e. Helping the convert understand the basic principles of the Christian life
   f. Seeing the convert learn to make exciting discoveries in personal Bible study
   g. Answering the convert's questions
2. The mechanics of follow-up. It is not easy to carry through your good intentions. You must be straightforward about the need for getting together. Then work hard to develop an agreeable format.
   a. *The time.* It is easier to meet with men early in the morning, with women in the early afternoon. When a married person becomes a Christian, follow-up should include his partner (probably during the evening).
   b. *The place.* A quiet restaurant is convenient for men when an early hour is agreed upon. Do not meet in a home unless both parties feel free to talk openly there.
   c. *The procedure.* General conversation, Bible study, prayer.
   d. *The subject matter.* A systematic study of a book of the Bible, Christian doctrine, or practical issues. Take time each week to answer questions.
3. Summary: four questions that determine the success of follow-up.
   a. Have you made a *friend* out of a convert?
   b. Is your new Christian friend able to see and talk about the centrality of his conversion?
   c. Is the convert growing in his appreciation of the Bible?
   d. Does your newly saved friend feel comfortable in the fellowship of the body of believers?

ASSIGNMENTS

1. Read each of the assurance verses referred to in this chapter.
2. Make a list of five Christians who have only recently become believers. Evaluate what you know of:
   a. How they were followed-up.
   b. What made the difference in each of their lives—why they are still going on with Christ.

3. Master at least one book on the subject of beginning the Christian life. Become familiar enough with the material that you can ask relevant questions of one who is studying it.

QUESTIONS FOR DISCUSSION

1. Do you think new Christians desire help from an older Christian on a regular basis?
2. Why are so many Christians unwilling to pay the price of one-on-one follow-up?
3. What can be done if the mate of a new believer is so antagonistic to Christianity that you are not welcome in that home?
4. What should you do if a person you lead to Christ has a personality type that clashes with yours?

PRAYER

Tell God what a joy it is to be His child and what a thrill it is to have spiritual children of your own. Ask that you may have the heart of God's Son, the Lord Jesus Christ, who knew that His Father had given Him spiritual sons and was determined that "of all which he hath given me I should lose nothing" (John 6:39). Ask God to help you to be the kind of person who makes it easy for a new believer to grow. And ask that you may see such a one as a friend and not just as a soul.

13

Corporate Follow-up—
A Task for the Church

There are two reasons why nothing about follow-up is easy. First, *follow-up depends on developing a unique life-style.* Successful follow-up is not just something you *do*: it is something you *are*. Second, *one needs help from the entire church family to succeed.* For when is follow-up successful? Only when an individual has become a part of the Christian community.

Like it or not, follow-up depends on *the kind of person you are* and *the kind of church with which you are united.* We have already discussed a strategy for discipling individuals on a one-on-one basis. But that is not the only issue in effective follow-up—your church is equally important. Salvation is a personal matter, but Christianity isn't. When a person is born again, he is born into a family. Every local church is but a partial attempt to bring visibility to this great invisible family of God.

One can be saved by himself, but no one can live the Christian life by himself. The apostle Paul says that individual Christians are like eyes and ears and hands of a body. That idea has tremendous implications for you as a potential evangelist. Everyone with an evangelistic heart should be part of a church that enjoys the following characteristics:

1. Sound, energetic Bible teaching by the pastor and church leaders;

2. A program geared to evangelism, follow-up, and training;

3. Warm, sincere friendship (so that you will never have to apologize to your visitor for the coldness of your church family);

You dare not separate follow-up from your church's life

173

4. A plan to make *every individual* feel cared for, necessary, and important to the work.

Many of us at the North Side Gospel Center have come of age since we began our evangelism training program several years ago. Originally, all of us were geared to expect growth through multiplication that would be so predictable you could calculate it with a slide rule. It hasn't happened. Believe me, it hasn't happened. Perhaps this is a comment on the kind of church we are or on the kind of pastor I am. I don't think so. Pastors I meet say the same thing. They engage in tough, lengthy spiritual warfare for every gain they make. Satan fights; the flesh resists. The story of our church's program is not all glorious. We have prayed and labored over souls we knew were wrestling with God. Our hearts break every time we see a prospect harden his soul against the things of God. Our experience was confirmed recently when evangelist Jack Murray visited our church. He said: "If you browse through a Christian bookstore and come across a book entitled *Evangelism Made Simple,* don't waste your money, for there is no easy way to evangelize."

Through it all we have matured. We don't anticipate the moon on a silver platter. But we do anticipate. The work of evangelism and follow-up is more difficult than we ever dreamed. It demands the mobilization of the entire church. This mobilization program is designed to enable us to realize three goals.

THREE GOALS OF LOCAL CHURCH FOLLOW-UP

ONE: THE GOAL OF HOLDING

The first goal of local church follow-up is holding. By *holding* we mean all activity that follows the initial meeting with the people we visit. We desperately want to keep meeting with them. That is why we have asked our callers to recognize a fundamental principle of visitation: *Don't visit anyone for whom you are not willing to assume personal responsibility for the rest of your life.* We say later that you were not designed to do for someone what only a body of believers can do. You were not designed to be intimately compatible with everyone. *But we believe that the person who has the joy of guiding a life into making a willful decision to trust Jesus Christ as Savior is responsible for introducing that newborn Christian to people who can help him grow.*

174

Here, then, is our precaution against everyone's responsibility becoming no one's responsibility. No matter whom a new Christian befriends, no matter how fast or slow his progress, we insist that those who first meet someone (and then see him converted) feel a sense of personal responsibility.

Gradually this commitment may be fulfilled entirely behind the scenes. It may involve prayer, purely casual friendship, and satisfaction at a distance as you see spiritual life grow. But even when your involvement is not open you will know what the apostle Paul sensed so long ago: "For though ye have ten thousand instructors in Christ, yet have ye not many fathers: for in Christ Jesus I have begotten you through the gospel" (1 Corinthians 4:15).

Will you consider this? Tell the Lord you are willing to *hold*—to keep meeting with—someone until he is part of a fellowship of believers or until he makes it evident that your company is no longer welcome.

Let's consider the implications of this for the various kinds of people you will be visiting:

1. *When people are impolite, hardened, or cold.* The Bible advises not to "cast ye your pearls before swine, lest they trample them under their feet" (Matthew 7:6). We want our precious hours to count. We believe that this is the end of the age. We do not want to waste time in these homes. But before we leave the homes of those who curse God, we remind them that "it is appointed unto men once to die, but after this the judgment" (Hebrews 9:27).

2. *When people are polite but not interested.* We maintain low-key, no-pressure associations with these people. They now know the gospel. We take pains to demonstrate its power through love. We invite them to special events and send them an occasional note. Every six months we visit them with the express purpose of sharing the entire gospel story.

3. *When people are interested but not ready to respond.* A small-group Bible study is in order. Perhaps, if you feel that they are not threatened by your presence, you might want to get together for a personal Bible study. Start in John. Then move to Romans (but only if you are studying together and can explain some of the theological terms in that epistle). Do not be afraid to invite such a one to church, but understand his reservations.

Have a plan in mind for each of these situations

Hardened people

Polite but not interested

Interested but not ready

175

Saved but bashful

Saved but immature

Saved and growing

Saved but can't attend church

4. *When people are saved but bashful.* All of us will meet people like these people. They need to be encouraged to worship regularly, but they must be introduced to a small group in which they feel free to participate. More about small-group Bible studies later.

5. *When people are saved but immature or superficial.* It's time for a strategic decision. Instead of spending hundreds of hours, literally years, in developing this individual's life, look for someone to take him under his wing. This is particularly important if there are only a few of you in your church who want to live on the cutting edge of evangelism. Pray that the Lord will bring to your mind just the right person. Go to him. Tell him that this can be his primary ministry.

6. *When people are saved and growing.* Don't waste a single year. Ask them to take this year's evangelism workshop training. Take them on evangelistic calls with you as soon as possible.

7. *When people are saved but cannot attend a sound church.* At best, this is a frustrating situation. Perhaps it involves a woman whose husband is adamantly opposed to her attending any church. It might be the situation of a teen or a young adult whose parents are vigorous adherents of a popular religious system. We have found that when we try hard enough there is almost always a way to plug such a person into fellowship with Christians. It may be radio, daytime Bible studies, correspondence courses, or some other opportunity. Pray about the matter. Be creative!

TWO: THE GOAL OF FOLDING

2. Folding: guiding a new believer into vital participation with a local church body

The second goal of local-church follow-up is folding. *Folding* has become popular with missiologists and evangelism strategists. Before I define it, I want to tell you some disquieting facts about mass evangelism. Studies of recent mass evangelistic campaigns show that only 2 percent of those who make some kind of profession become productively involved in the ongoing ministry of a local church. Moreover, in almost every case those who make up the 2 percent had an evangelical friend who led them into maturity. Whether we are willing to admit it or not, buckshot evangelism produces almost no fruit. Why? Because the Bible compares evangelism to seed planting:

"Behold, a sower went forth to sow; and when he sowed, some seeds fell by the way side, and the fowls came and devoured them up: some fell

176

upon stony places, where they had not much earth: and forthwith they sprung up because they had no deepness of earth: and when the sun was up, they were scorched; and because they had no root, they withered away. And some fell among thorns; and the thorns sprung up, and choked them: but other fell into good ground, and brought forth fruit, some an hundredfold, some sixtyfold, some thirtyfold" (Matthew 13:3-8).

This is a most illuminating parable. Our Lord Himself interprets it. Let's look at some fundamental lessons on evangelism and follow-up that are built into this parable:

The parable of the sower

1. The sower is scattering truth, not salvation. The seed is the word of the gospel.

2. Like all seeds, the seed of truth needs time to germinate. The sinner needs time to think about his condition and God's provision. Conviction through the unseen work of the Holy Spirit comes through a process that cannot be rushed.

It takes time

3. There are obstacles to overcome if the seed is to germinate. Satan stands by like a vulture, waiting to snatch up good seed (Mark 4:15). The stony ground represents a basis of superficial, emotional excitement (such as one might feel as he is caught up with the wonder of an evangelistic extravaganza of eighty thousand young people lifting their hands and singing "There's just something about that name"). The thorns stand for visible things that hinder a man's being able to view invisible things through the eye of faith. Like it or not, the battle rages as seed is sown. We must stand with the one who is the focal point of that battle.

There are obstacles

4. We have no right to make premature assumptions about a person's salvation. It is easy to equate an outward profession with genuine salvation. In fact, it is too easy. Our Lord Himself said that we should be conservative in our estimation of what happens as we sow seed. There is no way to get around it. The sign of reality is fruit. Conversion may well take place at the moment of one's first outward profession—but it didn't happen to me. What about you? The lesson is clear. We cannot let ourselves believe that our responsibility is over once a profession has been made.

The sign of reality: fruitfulness

Now, back to the task of defining *folding*. Basically it means to think of our evangelistic responsibility as a process rather than as an act. It is the process of taking a person who has no knowledge of truth, no fellowship with God's people, no involvement in a local church, and presenting

Definition of *folding*

177

to him the gospel, reinforcing this proclamation of truth with associations with other concerned Christians, guiding him into an understanding and profession of faith in Christ's work, and incorporating him into the fellowship, worship, and ministry of a local church. There's more to evangelism than we thought! It's not as easy as we thought. It's going to take more time than we thought.

But we must rethink evangelistic follow-up. It must be more than a package of literature for which people send in a free coupon. Again, here is our thesis: *evangelistic follow-up demands both a unique personal life-style and a unique style of local church ministry.*

THREE: THE GOAL OF MOLDING

3. Molding: bridging the gap between infancy and maturity

The third goal of local-church follow-up is molding. I have had the joy of seeing God change many lives in recent years. It is a wonderful sight. But the picture is not all roses. Some newborn believers live their entire lives as *newborn* believers. The writer of Hebrews understood this sad situation. He writes: "for when . . . ye ought to be teachers, ye have need that one teach you again which be the first principles of the oracles [Word] of God" (Hebrews 5:12). He continues: "Every one that useth milk is unskilful in the word of righteousness: for he is a babe" (Hebrews 5:13).

The goal of *molding* is to bridge the gap between infancy and maturity. It is a mistake to believe that progress toward maturity is automatic. When progress is rapid, it can usually be traced to three influences:

Three influences:

First, there is the influence of the Bible. We usually see a dramatic change in a person's disposition when he gets excited about the Bible. This excitement involves:

1. The Bible

1. The belief that he is capable of making rich *personal discoveries* about God in his own daily devotional time;

2. The opportunity to tell others about *those discoveries*—and listen to the discoveries of others—in a regularly scheduled but informal small group;

3. The exposure to solid, biblical exposition at corporate worship services. Excitement is generated by a weekly demonstration that there is more to the portion of Scripture being discussed than the person ever dreamed. As a result, he will want to go deeper and deeper into its treasures.

Second, there is the influence of fellow believers. Think about it. In your own experience, who has grown rapidly? Who never seems to grow at all? You will probably conclude that as long as a newborn believer seeks fellowship with an unsaved peer group, his growth will be retarded. When he begins to seek out Christian friends, his growth accelerates. Once again the influence of the body of believers ought to be threefold:

1. Each of us should look for somebody special. My children each want one good friend. Couples often develop a special relationship with another couple. As a pastor, I believe that one of the prime reasons new Christians leave a local church is that they cannot find one special person. *One friend* can transform a cold, impersonal church into a warm, friendly one overnight.

2. We all benefit from the opportunity to talk about burdens and blessings with a *small group* of people. That's why home Bible studies and church modules are appearing all over the country. Because they are caring groups of fewer than twenty people, they can help solve the problem of how a large church can effectively care for all its people.

3. The church as a body—that is, *the entire local fellowship*—ought to mean something special to each individual. We cultivate the notion that our church is a pretty special place and that meeting together on Sundays is a precious event.

Third, there is the influence of service. The last influence in the *molding* process is the discovery that God has something for me to do—right now—that can benefit others. Every believer can have a ministry and can be trained for more significant ministries from the first months of his new life. It is necessary that a church interested in *molding* practice the following:

1. Develop a spectrum of ministries that require little maturity or knowledge of the Word, such as bus driving, distributing literature, and so forth. (The trustees can be a great help here.)

2. Recruit newborn believers for training in evangelism immediately. There is no reason new Christians should not enroll in your next fourteen-week evangelism workshop.

3. Develop an understanding of what *means* lead to what *ends*. There is always confusion here. Teach loudly and frequently that God is primarily concerned with our faithfulness. Faithfulness in small things leads to open doors of opportunity in bigger things. On top of the list of immediate priorities is faithfulness in getting to

2. Fellow believers

3. Growth through service

know Jesus Christ better—that is, having a daily devotional time.

We have begun this chapter by listing three imperative goals in the follow-up process. They reveal the magnitude of the follow-up issue. There is much to be done. Let's review the three goals of follow-up:

1. *The goal of holding.* Every time we ring a doorbell we must recognize that few spiritual victories are instantaneous. We are beginning a new chapter of meetings with this home. We are beginning a process, not consumating an event.

2. *The goal of folding.* Evangelism must be seen as incomplete even after a profession of faith in Christ is made. The challenge is to see fruitfulness develop through personal meetings, exposure to truth, participation in a local fellowship of believers, and so forth.

3. *The goal of molding.* We must help the convert bridge the gap between infancy and maturity.

FOLLOW-UP AS PART OF A TOTAL CHURCH PROGRAM

Earlier in this chapter we listed the characteristics of a church that will succeed in holding on to its prospects and new believers: sound, energetic Bible teaching; a program geared to evangelism, follow-up, and training; warm, sincere friendship; and a plan to make every individual feel cared for, necessary, and important to the work. Let's look at the second of those components. How does a church gear itself for evangelism and follow-up? Consider these possibilities:

EVANGELISM-AND-VISITATION NIGHT

Churches must build evangelism into their weekly schedules

When no specific time in the week is designated for evangelism, it won't get done. This is universally true. Certainly individuals will win souls spontaneously, but no organized program will succeed if a regularly scheduled time slot is not blocked out for that purpose. Here are our goals:

1. We want to have every organization at our church represented on evangelism-and-visitation night. Every class, club, department, and organization is to have a visitation coordinator who is responsible for seeing to it that there are calls to make and that someone is there to make them.

2. We want to have a full complement of people on hand to make evangelistic calls every week of the year.

3. We want to have all twelve of our Young Adult Elders making calls each evangelism-and-visitation night—sometimes to new prospects, sometimes to members of their fellowship group.

4. We want to meet at 7:15 on evangelism-and-visitation night for a song, a prayer, a word of encouragement, and an assignment. Baby-sitting is provided at the church.

Again, we repeat: If you do not schedule a night for visitation and evangelism, it will not get done.

WEEKDAY YOUTH CLUBS

In many ways, our Awana clubs are the heart of our evangelism follow-up program.

1. All our Awana homes are visited twice a year by people in our evangelism workshop training program—more than six hundred families!

2. Awana leaders have huge demands placed upon them. They come to club night and they attend the midweek service with its prayer and planning time for each of our six Awana clubs. We ask them to participate in our Tuesday visitation night. Many of them cannot do so each week, but they can do it monthly.

3. Every Awana commander has a golden opportunity to see to it that his leaders are trained to witness to adults and that they are involved in visiting the homes of boys and girls regularly. Again, this *will not happen* if it is not incorporated into a weekly program.

4. Several times each year we have "Awana Nights" in our services. At those times we honor our clubbers and invite all the parents to attend. Many do.

SUNDAY SCHOOL

As a church grows to embrace several hundred people, it can no longer meet a basic need of each of us—intimacy. You cannot be intimate with hundreds. Wise is the Sunday school superintendent who understands that and concludes: "We are going to provide a fellowship group for everyone! By coming to class, people will not only learn to love the Word, they will also find an age grouping that will foster fellowship."

Using the age-grouping principle as a basis for Sunday school classes has become a very successful way of establishing "churches" within churches. In some of the large churches across the country, each adult class may have its own full-time minister. One thing is certain: *people*

Awana clubs

Age grouping in classes

181

thrive when they feel that someone cares for them. They hunger for a sense of belonging. They might express it like this: "I attend a church of ten thousand people, but the most wonderful thing about our church is that twenty-five of those people know my name!"

When Sunday school classes follow the age-grouping principle, they offer a church unlimited potential for evangelism and follow-up. The class itself can take an interest in new people and prospects. It can assign callers; it can offer social opportunities. The teacher of each class is a key person. He must be willing to promote calling on the church's visitation night.

Each class mobilized for outreach

SMALL FELLOWSHIP GROUPS

Often a church will have Sunday school classes that are still too large to meet individual needs. In such a situation the establishment of *fellowship groups* is in order. They may be called "cells" or "modules" or "action groups," but their purpose is the same. Last year our young adult class felt the need to establish fellowship groups within the framework of the larger class, which still meets as a unit on Sunday. The result has been very encouraging. We have found that this kind of group not only does a better job of caring and providing an opportunity for fellowship, but it is the key to follow-up as well. The following material was distributed to twelve key men when we began to prepare to divide our class into twelve fellowship groups. Reading it is the best way for you to understand our purposes.

Fact sheet about our fellowship groups

YOUNG ADULT FELLOWSHIP GROUPS

GOAL: Effective pastoral care of the Young Adult community. The development of groups small enough to provide intimacy, fellowship, and concern for each of the group's individual members.

METHOD: The geographical restructuring of the Young Adult community into twelve mini-congregations.

LEADERSHIP: Twelve selected Young Adult Elders: men who have a shepherd's heart, a love for the Word, and proven Christian character.

I. *Philosophy:*

A. These twelve mini-congregations are not to be seen merely as Bible studies.

182

Volunteer Bible studies usually minister only to the gregarious extrovert. The goal of these fellowship groups is to provide ministry to *everyone* and especially to the newcomer.

B. The Center Young Adult community could explode if the Young Adult Elders accept the responsibility of becoming involved in meeting the needs of approximately fifteen to twenty people.

C. From the Elder's standpoint, the key to this group is *caring*. From the people's standpoint, the key is *sharing*. We want all in these fellowship groups to feel that their group affords them a time to interact, share, pray, etc.

D. These groups must take the posture of *informal Bible studies where everyone's opinion carries the same weight*. Much of the success of these groups will depend on the leader's ability to bite his lip and assume a low profile.

E. We want each group to meet on a weekday evening (other than Tuesday and Wednesday), twice a month, with the Bible study sharing time from 7:30 p.m. to 8:30 p.m., with light refreshments following.

F. We want the married couples with children involved together so we ask each person in the group (men as well as women) to take a turn babysitting with all of the children present in a separate room or basement.

II. *Location and Distribution:*

A. Each fellowship group must meet in a home or apartment and cannot meet during the weekend.

B. We are going to break the Young Adult community into *area groupings*. This will give everyone a chance to fellowship with the Christians who live closest to him.

C. If a conflict arises (that is, a person cannot meet on the evening that his area group meets), he can meet with the fellowship group that is next closest to him.

D. Getting addresses of new folks and assigning them to a fellowship group will be the most crucial area of our new plan. Paul Kostelny (our class president) will be responsible for this and will notify each Elder about new folks who live in his geographical area.

E. When the number of people attending a

fellowship group exceeds twenty, that group must divide into two fellowship groups. A new Young Adult Elder will be selected by the twelve.

III. *Responsibilities of the Young Adult Elders:*

A. He is responsible for the simple mechanics of getting the group together. This involves arranging the time, place, etc., and relaying this information to the people in his group.

B. He is the *moderator* (but not necessarily the Bible teacher) of each group. Note: If these studies turn into just one more preachy "sit and listen" session, it will fail.

C. The Elder must see himself as the shepherd of his group, assisting the pastor in pastoral care. This may include such tasks as hospital visitation and personal counseling.

D. Perhaps the most crucial responsibility of all will be to meet with the other Young Adult Elders and the pastor once a month. This meeting will be on Sunday afternoons at 5:00 p.m. (fourth Sunday of the month). Here we can discuss issues that come up in our fellowship groups, pray about needs, and suggest key individuals we have come to know for various Center ministries (music, art, youth, drivers, etc.).

E. We ask for two week nights each week. Every Tuesday calls are to be made. Twice a month the groups will meet once a week night. We ask you to attend our mid-week service on the weeks your fellowship group does not meet.

IV. *Covenant of the Young Adult Elders:*

"I recognize that I am a sinner saved by grace. I am not perfect. Yet, I recognize that God is pleased to use imperfect people, people who are still fighting battles in their own lives to accomplish His work in the world. I rejoice to be able to have a part in that work. I know that the Bible says the elders are to 'feed the flock of God which is among you, taking the oversight of it, not by constraint but willingly. Not for filthy lucre, but of a ready mind. Neither as being lords over God's heritage, but being examples to the flock.' These verses speak of the three-fold ministry of eldership: *feeding, leading,* and *being.* As a man, I feel unequal to the task. But as a believer, I believe that the God who leads also enables. With my mind, I understand the responsibility of the Young Adult Elders. My heart feels challenged by this new avenue of service, and now with my will I commit myself to undertake this responsibility for the coming year as I am given grace from on high.''

Signed: _____

ADULT EVANGELISM GROUP

During the past generation, many churches have limited their evangelistic thrust to children. That is most unfortunate. Each church ought to have an organization that challenges, trains, and equips adults to reach adults. Our Crusaders (the members of our adult evangelism group) are simply those who have been trained in our evangelism workshops and are now training others and committing their Tuesday evenings to making evangelistic calls in the community.

Such a group must be a priority for every pastor. I do not consider myself an evangelist, but I believe that the great work of the church is evangelism. I want to fulfill my God-given responsibility to equip the saints for the work of the ministry. Note: *You cannot legislate evangelism by appointing a committee on evangelism.* Every committee on evangelism with which I have ever been acquainted has conceived of its task as arranging for an evangelist to come in and hold a series of meetings. That is not what the church needs today. It needs to recognize that God intended evangelism to spring forth *from within* the local body, not from without.

I am painfully aware that it is not easy to put together a group like our Crusaders. It demands the wholehearted support and enthusiasm of the pastor, who ought to be charter member number one of such a group. I do not believe that such a group will continue to exist over the years if the pastor is not its biggest encourager.

MAKING PEOPLE WELCOME

Before I close this chapter on the church's responsibility in evangelism and follow-up, let me mention just briefly some suggestions that will make follow-up easier because new people will believe that you are interested in them.

1. *Appoint friendly greeters.* We have discovered not only that greeters are a blessing to church guests, but also that each Sunday school class should have greeters standing at the classroom door. Greeters should have as a prime concern the securing of names and addresses in the church's guest book.

The Crusaders

You cannot legislate evangelism

How can we organize to welcome our visitors warmly?

1. Appointing greeters

185

2. Introducing visitors

3. Training to entertain

4. Knowing what to do with names and addresses

5. Mobilizing

6. Getting new people interested in training

7. Having an evangelistic emphasis at a specific service

2. *Introduce people in church.* Have them stand up, give their names, and tell where they are from. Then have your ushers alerted to give them a booklet and a visitor's registration card. This need not be embarrassing in the slightest. People will be glad that you care.

3. *Train your people to entertain.* This is the best of all possible follow-up procedures. My wife and I have developed an inviolable proposition: *our relationship is never the same again toward people who have joined us for fellowship around our dining room table.* We suggest that each month our people entertain someone they don't know.

4. *Know precisely what you are going to do with names and addresses.* Here is our procedure. Names and addresses of visitors are given to our church secretary. She makes up four copies. One goes to me (I write a welcome letter). One goes to our visitation pastor. One goes to the head of our Tuesday visitation program (here comes another Crusader visit!). Finally, the name is given to a Young Adult Elder for a personal visit or to one of the other adult Sunday school teachers.

5. *Mobilize.* Recruit your prospects into the next evangelism workshop. We have seen folks saved in the workshop training itself. This is an ideal way to ground a person in the central facts of Christianity. Encourage individuals who have made a decision to trust Jesus Christ as their Savior to get involved in your church's evangelism training program as soon as possible.

6. *Offer significant training in evangelism at least twice each year.* Again, there is no finer way to acquaint a new believer with the great issues of the gospel. Never permit newborn believers to think of evangelism as odd, extracurricular, or only for the spiritually mature.

7. *Gear one of your Sunday services toward evangelism.* We have trained our people to know that there will be an explanation of the gospel and an opportunity to respond to it at our Sunday evening service. We still preach an expositional message to Christians, but we are well aware that at almost every service unsaved people are listening for the first time. Our Crusaders are prepared to counsel with all who respond to the gospel invitation.

A closing comment: Home Bible studies come and go. New believers can wander around for years—traveling from study to study—and never grow. I know of no one who can thrive in his Christianity and ignore the vehicle God ordained to reach the world—the local, visible church. Don't be ashamed of your church. Don't apologize for inviting newborn believers to come to your church. If your church is geared to evangelism, sound preaching, and warm fellowship, you will be doing your new friend an exquisite favor. It's fantastic to be part of a family!

Don't be ashamed of your church

REVIEW OF CHAPTER 13
CORPORATE FOLLOW-UP—
A TASK FOR THE CHURCH

Successful follow-up depends on what kind of person you are (you have a unique life-style) and what kind of church you attend (no one can live the Christian life by himself). Therefore, anyone who is serious about evangelism ought to be serious about his church. It ought to have these characteristics: sound, energetic Bible teaching; a program geared to evangelism, follow-up, and training; warm, sincere friendship; a plan to make every individual feel special—cared for.

1. Three goals of local church follow-up
    a. *Holding*—No matter what the outcome of a visit to a home—even if a profession of faith is made—a new relationship is a tenuous thing. It must be guarded, tendered, nurtured. We must see such a visit as only the beginning of a process, never as an end to itself.
    b. *Folding*—We must never conclude that evangelism has been successful until a new believer is in the fold—enjoying the fellowship of the family of believers and in turn making a contribution of service to that body.
    c. *Molding*—We must bridge the gap between infancy and maturity. This is accomplished through three influences:
        (1) The Bible (the key to any dramatic growth)
        (2) Fellow believers (when one's close friends are Christians, growth accelerates)
        (3) Service (new believers thrive under the challenge of being trained to serve)
2. Follow-up as part of a total church program
    Key: Every activity and organization in the church contributes to this great process.
    a. Weekly visitation night—No organized attempt at evangelism will succeed without a specified time for calls of all varieties: prospecting, follow-up, caring for Christians.
    b. Weekday youth clubs—Not only are they a blessing for youth, they are also a wonderful stepping-stone into homes.
    c. Sunday school—In larger churches, age-group classes enable everyone to be cared for. Each class has great opportunities to fellowship with new believers.
    d. Small fellowship groups—There is no better way to combine evangelism, follow-up, and training. These groups are the wave of the future.
    e. Adult evangelism group—The people in this group are trained to present the gospel to strangers anywhere. They make calls on prospects every week.
    f. Making people feel welcome—The church that accomplishes this will grow.

ASSIGNMENTS

1. Carefully evaluate the potential of your church for attracting new believers. Be positive in this evaluation. Do not stress what you are doing wrong. Instead, stress what has worked already and can be improved in the future.
2. Make an appointment to see your pastor. Tell him that you are excited about being available—at his disposal—to develop your church's resources for evangelism, follow-up, and training. You will find that he is more concerned than you are! Ask him to tell you about his dreams toward those ends. Then discuss how his dreams might become realities.

QUESTIONS FOR DISCUSSION

1. Why don't most churches divide their membership into small fellowship groups? What are the obstacles to overcome? The dangers to face?
2. Discuss this principle: Don't visit anyone for whom you are not willing to assume personal responsibility for the rest of your life. Is that asking too much? What does "responsibility" mean?
3. Why are so many pastors and church leaders concerned about the goal of folding rather than just about holding impersonal evangelistic meetings?
4. What is your Sunday school doing that is successfully drawing new believers into the fellowship?

PRAYER

Thank God for making you a part of a local body of believers. Acknowledge that the body cannot grow unless its many members work together to produce growth. Tell God that you want to have a part in that growth, and ask Him to reveal to you His will for you in this matter. Thank God for your church—for its people and for its leadership. Ask Him to unite your hearts as you confess that you need each other if you are going to accomplish the great task of reaching the lost and loving them into the fellowship.

14

Where Do We Go from Here?

I have heard more than one preacher conclude his morning message with these words: "Beloved, this brings us to the end of *worship,* and the beginning of *service!*" Not bad theology at all. If I have been praying about anything during the weeks that I have been writing this manual, it has been this: "Lord, do not allow anyone to read this book and then close it after he is finished without its forcing him to make changes in his life and thinking."

Come to some conclusions

Many people have read books on evangelism. I have an entire shelf in my library for books on evangelism. It was not until several years ago, when I determined that I was going to *do* something about evangelism, that life became interesting. You must make some decisions now. Tomorrow this book will adorn your shelf and you will have forgotten the proddings of the Spirit if you do not come to some conclusions now. This is serious business. I wish I could speak to you in person right now.

At the beginning of our workshop series, I ask the leader of our evangelism group (the Crusaders) to take a few minutes to tell the people taking evangelism training that our training program is only the first step, that it can lead to something bigger—something permanent. He tells the people that he wants them to consider two commitments: first, that they give their Tuesday nights for the coming year to evangelism; second, that they consider joining Crusaders, with its many activities and its monthly planning meetings.

Two commitments:
1. Give Tuesday evenings for evangelism
2. Join Crusaders

There is one more crucial point in our training program, one more place where a person must come to a conclusion. It takes place during the fifth week of training. At that time, I ask the leader

190

of our Tuesday outreach to say a few words at the beginning of class. This is what he says: "Several weeks ago you were each asked to consider two long-term objectives. I hope you are still praying about them. My burden is much more immediate. I have just one short-term goal. That is to see each of you come back next week when we launch out into people's homes for the first time. You will all be amazed at how many "legitimate" excuses for skipping the meeting next week will come up between now and then. Satan will be on your back constantly. But don't let anything stop you. You have come too far to turn back now. Unless you see this gospel message at work in the homes of unsaved people, it will never become a part of your life. It will never turn you into the dynamic, witnessing Christian that God intended you to be."

You are in a very similar circumstance. You have given cursory attention to a plan for telling others about the gospel of the grace of God. *Where do you go from here?* I have two suggestions. *First,* at the very least find an evangelism partner and begin to reread this book slowly. Do every assignment, face every question at the end of each chapter, memorize every verse of Scripture. Then, by all means, go together into people's houses. Learn by the trial-and-error method. Remember, this is not a short-term thing. Make a commitment to each other that you will stay with it for at least a year. *Second,* determine to do all that is in your power to bring a training program into your church's corporate life. Encourage your pastor or minister of evangelism to read this manual. It is absolutely necessary to have the unqualified support of the pastor if an evangelistic training program is to have a permanent, profound impact on a church.

As you consider this possibility, I want to give you a more comprehensive picture of our own program of evangelistic training. You will see its many weaknesses as well as its strengths.

But before I do, let me tell you something very important. The key to any evangelistic outreach is a *person.* No program succeeds without a person to bring it to life. No training will last unless a person commits himself to seeing it through dark days. It is breathtaking to see what happens when someone allows the evangelistic imperative of Jesus Christ to become an irresistible force in his life. May God grant every pastor the privilege of working with men who say: "The gospel is

Where do you go from here?

1. An evangelism partner

2. Lead your church into a training program

It begins with one person

worthy of every ounce of energy, time, and sacrifice that I can ever make. I *will* be trained. I *will* do all that is in my power to implement an evangelistic training program in my church. The issues are too important. Nothing—*nothing*—must interfere." The key to the potential for evangelism in every church in America today is one person. One person. I must ask, *is that person you?*

THE DEVELOPMENT OF OUR EVANGELISM PROGRAM

You ask: Has the program you are describing turned your church into a cathedral of thousands? No. We are still relatively small. Yet I believe that we have several hundred of the most dedicated and best trained young adults in the country. I mention this because I want you to believe that you can have a workable program in your church. We are just like you. We have few professional people in our congregation; we have little material wealth; we come from all over a large metropolitan area. We have a homely building, inadequate parking, and a merely average preacher. But our evangelism program is working. Yours can too.

THE BURDEN OF MY HEART

Several years ago, the Lord put an inescapable burden on my heart for a training program. The key to the program had to be a fresh way in which to present the gospel of grace. Everywhere I went, pastors and evangelists told their people to give their hearts to Christ, but there was no gospel. I was constrained to create a program that could teach people how to present Christ in the way that my heart cried out that salvation ought to be presented. The program had to have three components: First, it had to major in the essential issues of salvation. Second, it had to feature on-the-job training. And third, it had to lead to something more—something regular and permanent.

Announcements were made. Several people with open hearts and minds but little knowledge about such a program were stirred. We set a date for the first workshop. I locked myself in my study and began to prepare some notes. Those first notes were hopelessly inadequate, but the nucleus of a strategy began to develop. Dr. James Kennedy's book *Evangelism Explosion* (Wheaton, Ill.: Tyndale, 1970) was a wonderful help to me, especially in the areas of discerning spiritual needs and presenting assurance.

The same gospel . . . a fresh presentation

192

THE FIRST WORKSHOP BEGINS

It was an encouraging but definitely inauspicious beginning. About thirty brave souls showed up. None of us really knew what he was doing. But we learned fast. Soon, we began to see dropouts. Fear was taking its toll. Curiosity-seekers no longer returned. The group was shrinking in size and growing in grace.

The people who remained wrote feverishly in their little ten-page workbook. New ideas came to me. Many were suggested by the people themselves. Then came the night we made our first calls. We were all scared. We had no trainers. We were the trainers and the trainees! Then someone was saved. The ice was broken. That original group solidified. They are the backbone of our present program.

THE CRUSADERS COME INTO BEING

After the first workshop, we felt an immediate responsibility to provide a channel for the evangelistic energies of those who had completed the training. A group called the Crusaders was formed. By definition, "the Crusaders are the adult evangelistic arm of our church. They are men and women who have graduated from our evangelism workshop and who now meet regularly to create and implement a strategy to reach our area with the gospel of Christ. At first we met irregularly. Then we met on the last Friday of the month. Ultimately, we moved to Tuesday nights so that we could reinforce in our minds the fact that *Tuesday means evangelism.*

Crusaders

The Crusaders organization has had ups and downs. Now we know that its downs just provide opportunities for God to work in a fresh way. During one dry spell, I asked nine of our key men to meet with me in a motel room for a night of prayer. I shall never forget that night. We saw things change visibly from that night forward. God met us. We were moving again. We found our direction.

What kinds of projects have the Crusaders undertaken? Absolutely first on the priority list is the regular Tuesday-night program of evangelism. The Crusaders make hundreds of calls each year. They become the trainers for those Tuesday evenings of on-the-job training during our workshops. Here are some of their other projects: They sponsor an evangelistic film, concert, or banquet each month at the church; they sponsor weekly and monthly street meetings at the airport, shopping

Mass evangelism

centers, beaches, and forest preserves; they sponsor special evangelistic crusades; they plan neighborhood canvasses, door-to-door evangelistic thrusts, and literature-distribution days; they write articles in local newspapers; they plan a strategy to reach our city for Christ through mass media; they sponsor a telephone counseling service; they organize summer flea-market witnessing; they serve as counselors as people make public decisions at our services; they organize special activities, like rallies in downtown plazas, films on local college campuses, and so forth; they provide significant follow-up concern for all who come to know Christ.

THE SECOND WORKSHOP BEGINS

It became clear to us that we had begun something that must not ever be allowed to grind to a halt. We decided to hold a fourteen-week training program each spring and fall. Almost one hundred people attended each of them. The second workshop taught us many lessons. For example, we didn't have nearly enough trainers and we were haphazard in our attendance procedures. During that workshop we began to see a need for *certification*. We decided that in order to become certified, one must not miss more than three of the workshop sessions, he must not miss more than one week of on-the-job training, and he must have his assignments and memory work completed.

Certification

Those who are certified receive a *fishhook* lapel pin, which has come to be the symbol of our Crusaders group. More than a hundred of our young adults now wear a fishhook pin with pride. Many people from other churches wear them as well. (This spring, people from eight local churches are taking the training.) Everyone who is certified is put on a master list by one of our secretaries. He is then notified about future Crusader activities and urged to become a trainer when the time of the next workshop draws near. Those who complete our training are recognized and certified in front of the entire congregation. We want everyone to know that we as a local church congregation are totally behind this program.

Key laymen responsible

Another lesson we learned is that one man is needed to take the administrative burden off the pastor's back. This man's main job is to provide prospects each week for our Crusaders to visit and to come up with a hundred new prospects for each of the five nights of the workshop series, when we visit homes in our neighborhood.

The second workshop also saw a need for professionalism and consistency. Now we expect our trainers to stay with one trainee for the entire program. In that way he becomes responsible for seeing that the trainee does not drop out. We have upgraded our manuals as well. We want people to master the gospel of grace excellently.

THE THIRD WORKSHOP

Nearly one hundred began our third worshop—but fewer than seventy survived. Our constant prayer is that God will teach us how to eliminate dropouts. People are so busy. Anyone can find an excuse. With the coming of our third workshop, we expanded our secretarial staff. One secretary gives herself to making out prospect cards and following up on assigned calls. Another secretary has become the much appreciated follow-up secretary. Still another secretary does the attendance and record keeping for the workshop itself.

Secretarial help

The graduation of the third group was one of the most electric services we ever had at our church. All the people who were to receive certificates came up on the platform with their trainers—a hundred strong. Many gave testimonies. I gave out their fishhook pins. Those little lapel pins have come to represent a great deal.

WHERE WE STAND TODAY

As I am writing this chapter we are in the midst of our fourth major workshop series. People from eight nearby churches are giving up their Tuesday nights to attend. So many of the people have encouraged me to expand our workshop notes into a manual that the words you are now reading are the result.

We are now considering another giant step. We are considering putting a man on our pastoral staff who would function as pastor at large in charge of Crusader ministries. He could train people from other churches, at their churches, five nights a week. He could call on people from many churches to participate in citywide projects that are not originated at our church. It is exciting to think big thoughts about the future.

One thing I know for sure about my own future is that I will always be teaching the gospel of grace each spring and fall. It is the most satisfying aspect of my entire pastoral ministry. It is the key to growth by multiplication. If I am the only one leading people to Christ, our church can grow only by addition. But if I can train others to witness, we can grow the New Testament way—by multiplication. Acts 6:1 says: "When the number of the disciples was multiplied." That's it. That's what I want.

Our strengths

THE KEYS TO OUR EVANGELISM PROGRAM

Again let me say that we are not a superchurch. Far from it. The pastor is ordinary. The people are just like you. If there are reasons our work is growing and our evangelism program is effective, they probably include the following:

1. Confidence in God

1. *We have unshakable confidence in a miracle-working God.* Without that confidence, we would all be scared. The key verse of the Crusaders is: "With men it is impossible, but not with God: for with God all things are possible" (Mark 10:27). If God is alive, we ought to expect the miracle of conversion. He is at work in people's hearts.

2. Confidence in the message

2. *We have absolute confidence in our message.* We are constantly accused of being intolerant and picky. Not so. We simply insist that any solid presentation of the gospel center on what Christ did for us on the cross. We are jealous for that. We believe that each of the three crucial issues in evangelism must be clearly presented: first, that all men are sinners and that sin separates from God; second, that Calvary is God's only provision for man's sin; and third, that saving faith is claiming by personal choice and relying exclusively upon the work of Christ on the cross to be sufficient payment for one's sins.

What strength we draw from that message. It is dynamic. The gospel works—we don't. There is indescribable strength in knowing that your message is true and that it is the only power in the universe that can transform lives.

3. Manual that provides form and flexibility

3. *We have a flexible yet clear-cut manual.* Our manual is very basic. Yet it is uncompromising. I trust that the book you are reading is much the same in spirit as the live presentations that I give in class. We give everyone the right to put his own personality into his witnessing. Many personalities, many different illustrations—yet one message.

More and more we see a need for precision in any training program. That is why at the outset

196

we stress clearly defined objectives, precision in memory work, and completion of all assignments.

4. *We have certification—in a tangible form.* Incentives are a part of life. It is especially important to offer incentives in a voluntary program like ours. We offer a negative and a positive incentive to continue. The negative is attendance enforcement. On the positive side, we present the fishhook pin as a symbol of accomplishment to all who complete our training. Believe me, those of us who have endured the rigors of the course wear our pins with great satisfaction.

5. *We have the Crusaders.* This has been a great boon to our program. The Crusaders are the crux of our ongoing program. Everyone in the training program is being "propagandized" to become a Crusader upon graduation. This is the outgrowth of our commitment to the principle that our basic workshop is only the first step in a life-style geared to evangelism. This group is also the key to our ongoing Tuesday night visitation program.

6. *We set apart Tuesday nights for evangelism.* All our regular evangelistic endeavors are geared for Tuesday nights. We still have special concerts and films on the weekends, but our training and door-to-door ministries, as well as the Crusader meetings, are all scheduled for Tuesdays. This has put us into a Tuesday night habit. It's become automatic. None of us knows what is on television on Tuesdays. We spend *every* Tuesday at church. Now the whole church plans its schedule so as to avoid a Tuesday conflict.

7. *We have exposure before the entire church.* Here's where I come in. I schedule our services. Thus I have the opportunity to encourage our congregation to get excited about the things that excite me. I make regular pulpit announcements about Crusader activities, ask various people to say a word to the fellowship, and give the Crusaders time in our services to tell about their burden for souls. Also, our new recruits are always certified in public services.

8. *We have a weekday Awana program to provide parents to visit.* More than five hundred young people visit our facilities each week via our six Awana clubs. Those clubs provide us with an almost limitless number of parents, who become the heart of our visitation program. We feel a great responsibility to reach the families of our Awana kids. If parents don't become Christians during the years in which their children come to

4. Certification

5. Crusaders

6. Tuesday nights set apart

7. Exposure before the church

8. Weekday youth program

our clubs, we know that there is but a slim chance that their youngsters will stick with us.

In a previous chapter, we discussed the value of having a reason to make a visit to a home. Time after time, people greet us with suspicion as they open the door. But as soon as they learn of our purpose—to tell them the purpose of our Awana clubs, of which their children are members—they open their doors to us. I have never met a parent who did not appreciate what we are trying to do for his children.

9. Refusal to get discouraged

9. *We refuse to get discouraged.* Ask any pastor—the hardest program in the church to maintain throughout the years is evangelism. As our workshops began to grow and we became increasingly excited about the quality of our training, we sent representatives to neighborhood churches, asking them if their people might like to participate. We got the same answer repeatedly: "Oh, we had our own evangelism training program—once." But once is not enough. I know of no exceptions to this rule: *Every church that sponsors a successful evangelism program succeeds because one person or perhaps a small group of people refuse to get discouraged.* That's the key.

My life was changed when I attended a Moody Pastors' Conference. In rubbing shoulders with a thousand pastors, I was shocked by much of what I saw. I overheard conversations of men who were whipped. Others took heart in the fact that there were more pulpits than men to fill them. I saw men who viewed the ministry as a way to make a living. But I thank God that I also saw a few men who were hungry to make things happen in their communities. At that conference, an overwhelming passion came over me as my heart cried: "Lord, you have called me to the most exciting undertaking the world has ever known! The moments of life are few. Please give me the grace *to make things happen* in the lives of the people I touch. Use me to effect a change in the outlook of every human being I meet. Lord Jesus Christ, you want things to happen in human lives. You live in me. You have commanded me to reign over my own life, to seize control over circumstances rather than be dominated by them. Use me to affect the destinies of men. Help me to believe that one man who is hungry enough can change the destiny of a city like Chicago. Lord, help me to be faithful in the minute details of life, but never again allow me to live a day without dreaming big dreams. Finally, Lord, *give me the grace to refuse to become discouraged."*

A short time later, I got a letter from well-known author and Bible teacher Craig Massey. The last sentence was this: "Dick, refuse to get discouraged!" He's right, and that truth was evidenced in his ministry.

At every critical juncture, there have been disappointments. Trainers don't show up. We have many dropouts over our fourteen-week period. People who complete our training don't become part of our regular Tuesday visitation program. The weather is rotten! People aren't home! Our baby-sitter is sick. Do you know *Murphy's Law*? "If something can possibly go wrong, it will." Amen! That's the first half of the story of our evangelism program. The second half of the story is that God has given us a few dedicated men and women who won't quit. I get a lump in my throat when I think of those people. They thrill me. You don't know their names, but they are giants of the faith.

Recently I heard a preacher define faith as it is used in Hebrews 10:35-37 as *toughness*. I like that. The spiritual commandos at our church are those who have become tough enough to hang in there because they believe the promises of God.

10. *We have key people to form a nucleus.* Our program could not work if God did not give us the right people to make it work. The pastor must be one of those committed to an evangelistic training program. He must *advertise and glamorize* it from the pulpit. Then the lay leaders of the church must become involved. Of the hundred in our work who are certified, of the fifty who make calls on Tuesdays, of the scores who have helped us as trainers—not one person receives a dime in remuneration. They have big hearts, giant burdens for lost people, and huge faith in God.

10. A dedicated nucleus

11. *We have attendance incentives.* Our program has the same problem others have. The primary one is the refusal of people to face their fears. Thus, on the fifth week of class—when we go into homes for the first time—we lose lots of participants. We combat this tendency in several ways. First, we insist that no one who wants to be certified miss more than three weeks. Second, we employ a secretary who calls those who miss several workshops. Third, we assign one trainer to one trainee for the entire workshop. The trainer, therefore, has the responsibility of making sure that his trainee finishes the program.

11. Attendance incentives

12. Refresher courses

12. *We have refresher courses.* All of us tend to wander away from a structured presentation. We allow our personalities to show through. That is good, but not when the objective is to teach a trainee a fixed presentation. Therefore, we review the basics with all of our graduates at least once each year. Also, we have an advanced evangelism workshop each winter for all who are certified.

13. Pride in our church

13. *We have pride in our church.* Never start a program in a church you cannot support with your whole heart. Ask yourself this question: If someone brought me to the service last week for the first time, would I be impressed? I'm so blessed. Four years ago I inherited a forty-year tradition of pride in our church. That pride continues. Its an awful thing to have to apologize for your church. To the degree that you are persuaded that your church is important, your feelings will be perceived by others. We are not ashamed of our Savior, our message, or our fellowship. We believe that God can use our church to evangelize a city. We are working toward that end with all our strength. You must either support your church with all your might or find another.

Our weaknesses

THE WEAKNESSES OF OUR PROGRAM

I include the following paragraphs to encourage you. We have lots of weaknesses in our program! (Somehow, people are relieved to discover that other people have weaknesses.) We are not proud of our weaknesses, but we recognize their existence. We pray about them regularly. If your church begins a training program, you may well encounter the same problems we do:

1. Too many dropouts

1. *We have too many dropouts.* We operate at a staggering mortality rate of nearly 50 percent. At this point, I can think of only two suggestions that we haven't already implemented: Get a better teacher or charge an exorbitant tuition fee (which causes people to stay simply because they want their money's worth!).

2. Trainers of uneven quality

2. *We have trainers of uneven quality.* Every trainer is unique. Some of our people are outstanding. Others leave something to be desired. Our thesis is that it is better to take each trainee out witnessing fewer times and then use him to teach others than it is to use unsatisfactory trainers. We are moving toward the day when we can be very selective in the trainers we use. By the way, men trainers work with men, women with women.

200

3. *We have big city logistics.* When I was a pastor in Nebraska, the nearest stoplight was seventeen miles away. In Chicago, we have seventeen stoplights for each mile. People visit our church from a twenty-mile radius. The problems of logistics are obvious. It is discouraging to drive for an hour only to find that your prospects are not home. Sometimes we make calls in dangerous neighborhoods. When that is the case, those calls are made only by men.

4. *We have limited age-group participation.* Perhaps it is because I am a young man and the key leaders of our training program are young adults, but we have not succeeded in training the bulk of our congregation that is over forty. Those people have been slow to get involved in this ministry. This may be due to a conviction that they already know how to tell others about their faith. It may be due to the fear of attempting a new thing. Possibly some of these people believe that evangelism is young people's work!

5. *We have confusion about how to take our training program beyond our church.* We want to be used to train individuals from other churches. A dozen of our best Crusaders have committed themselves to teach our program in other churches one night a week if pastors invite them. When people from other churches attend the program at our church, we invite them to supply us with the names of people from their church. We then ask those people if they would like to take the training.

Here is the problem. We are convinced that training must lead to a permanent commitment regarding evangelism. There seem to be three possibilities available: First, those certified from other churches could establish training programs in their own churches. (We are happy to supply teachers.) Second, those certified could work with evangelism partners on their own—not as part of a church sponsored program—and make calls on people to whom God leads them. Or third, everyone who has been trained in evangelism could become part of a nondenominational thrust to reach strategic areas of the city with the gospel (literature campaigns, street meetings, concerts, campus rallies, shopping center thrusts, airport evangelism, and so forth).

Some pastors fear that if people come to our church for training they might not come back home. We urge those pastors to develop a training program in their own churches. Yet we affirm

201

that our goal in this workshop program is not to steal sheep; our goal is to train them.

6. *We have unrealistic expectations.* Here is our biggest failing. Come back with me into my thoughts of two years ago. I was enamored with the thought of *growth by multiplication.* My expectations ran along these lines: *This spring we train twenty-five; then next fall those twenty-five train twenty-five more; then next spring those fifty together train fifty; then those one hundred together train one hundred; then those two hundred together train two hundred; then those four hundred together. . . .*

It hasn't worked that way. Only a fraction of any one graduating class discover that they have a special gift and a special passion for evangelism. Our growth comes slowly. We may never exceed a hundred trainees. Only time will tell. Yet even though our expectations have not been realized, I am blessed with more people making more visits to more homes than any other pastor in Chicago.

HOW TO BEGIN AN EVANGELISM PROGRAM OF YOUR OWN

I want to conclude this manual by urging you to pray about your role in fulfilling the Great Commission. Some who are trying to fulfill this commission are doing so by techniques that violate scriptural principles. Yet I thank God for *everyone* who is at least doing what he believes is necessary to see the church of Jesus Christ completed. It's time for you to make some decisions. Could God use you to introduce an evangelism workshop program into your church? Here are some suggestions:

1. *Master this manual yourself.* Learn word perfect the three crucial issues in evangelism, the five great truths about the gospel, the key questions to ask, the most vivid illustrations, the bridges of transition that make your presentation smooth and logical, and, finally, memorize the key Scripture verses. Now ask yourself: Has the program helped me? If the answer is no, don't try to begin this program in your church.

2. *Find one person who shares your heart for souls.* Become an evangelistic team. Train each other. Begin to pray for an evangelistic burden in your church.

3. *Talk to your pastor.* Give him a copy of this manual. Tell him about our program. Suggest that he write to me, Pastor Dick Sisson, Middleton Baptist Church, 6101 University Avenue, Madi-

202

son, Wisconsin 53705. Suggest that several from your church visit one of our Tuesday night workshops. Ask your pastor to pray about his role in training people for the great task of evangelism.

Start your
workshop

4. *With the blessing of your pastor (in fact, it may very well be the pastor who is selected), choose a teacher for your first workshop.* Select a convenient night. Prepare your material. Invite people publicly, but talk to key individuals in your church personally.

5. *Establish guidelines for certification.*

6. *Begin to establish a list of prospects who can be visited in the coming weeks.* As soon as possible, turn over this time-consuming task to a competent secretary.

Start on a high
note

7. *Start on a high note.* Our first workshop session is highlighted by a taped recording of Dr. James Kennedy's personal testimony of how he became a trainer of soul-winners.

8. *Plan for the next step.* We urge you to implement the two "next steps" we use. From the very first night of your training program, begin to urge your people to consider two commitments: First, ask them to consider committing each Tuesday night to evangelism. Soon your church will have a thriving visitation night. Second, ask them to become part of a local church organization (like our *Crusaders*) that is committed to meeting regularly to develop and implement an evangelistic strategy for reaching your community with the gospel.

Major in the
message of grace

9. *Revel in the gospel of grace.* Here is your power, your glory. You are saved freely, by God's grace, because of Christ's blood, simply because you believe the gospel. It may seem to be too good to be true, but it *is* true. Marvel in this message. Exult in your salvation. Never stop glorying in the meaning of Calvary.

10. *Refuse to become discouraged.* Yes, you will have dropouts also. You will not find people at home. It may rain every time you plan to ring doorbells. But refuse to get discouraged.

11. *Remember that we want to help you in any way we can.* Our goal is to provide evangelistic training for anyone who wants it. It is our prayer that we may soon be able to put someone on our staff who will give his undivided attention to directing our own Crusaders and to teaching training programs to other congregations all around the country.

Get stirred up

12. *Get stirred up.* Remember these precious quotations:

All things are possible!

"We will have all eternity to enjoy our crowns, but only a few brief moments on earth in which to win them."

"I want to be a fork in the road so that when a man gets to me he must go one way or the other!" (Jim Elliott).

"With men it is impossible, but not with God: for with God all things are possible" (Mark 10:27).

"They that sow in tears shall reap in joy. He that goeth forth and weepeth, bearing precious seed, shall doubtless come again with rejoicing, bearing his sheaves with him" (Psalm 126:5-6).

Moody Press, a ministry of the Moody Bible Institute, is designed for education, evangelization, and edification. If we may assist you in knowing more about Christ and the Christian life, please write us without obligation: Moody Press, c/o MLM, Chicago, Illinois 60610.

Notes

Notes

Notes

Notes